IT'S
NOT
ABOUT
THE BOOK!

Why most authors don't make money

David Gil Cristóbal
Chris & Karene Lambert-Gorwyn

Exclusive Offer

We would love for you to get the most out of this book and along with all the great content contained in these pages, we have some additional training materials and support lined up for you.

Visit www.hcbpublishing.com/book/offers to access additional free support and training and a FREE Book Strategy Session with our Coaching Team valued at over £1,000!

We wrote this book to help you succeed!

Visit this Webpage now and let's make that happen together!

www.hcbpublishing.com/book/offers

Best-Selling & Award-Winning Authors

David Gil Cristóbal and Chris & Karene Lambert-Gorwyn

Preface by Raymond Aaron | New York Times best-selling author

© 2022 - 1st edition

The Legal Bit

HCB Publishing Ltd.
London | United Kingdom
Printed in EU, UK, Canada and the United States of America
ISBN: 978-1-8380061-2-9

We dedicate this book to all the doers, dreamers and positive crazies who make our world a little better, day by day.

Great goals are not naive, but worth striving for.

Without you, our lives would be less colourful - and this book would not have been written.

Preface

You can do it, if you only believe that you can. You control your destiny and with it your success!

There are many things you cannot control, but you can control two things that really matter - your mind and your attitude. External forces have little to do with success. Therefore, if you programme yourself for success, you will find a way to achieve it even in the most difficult circumstances. Solutions to most problems come from one source and one source only:

From yourself

Approaching life with all your might is like navigating rapids in white water on a small rubber raft. Once you decide to do it and plunge into the waters, it becomes difficult to turn around and paddle back upstream to calmer waters.

But it's exactly this excitement and adventure that makes it all worthwhile. You will probably never know the depths of despair if you never make the attempt, but neither will you experience the incredible happiness of success.

Decide to take control of your life. You are only one book away from success. Get started! The world is waiting for you and your success book.

Raymond Aaron
New York Times best-selling author

Contents

INTRODUCTION

Introduction

Books are uniquely portable magic - Stephen King

Increasingly, we are all becoming experts. With the information age, the all pervasive impact of technology and more and more people turning away from traditional employment, or at least developing a side hustle, it sometimes feels like everyone is an expert in something. Throughout history, there have always been experts, the local midwife or wise woman, the farmer who had the best crops, teachers who managed to have more success than others with their class, star coaches, craftspersons, businesspersons, world leaders and many more. However, with the advent of more accessible technology and ways of sharing or demonstrating our expertise with a wider audience, it certainly feels like there are just more 'experts' in the world.

This brings challenges and questions. If everyone is an expert, how do you stand out? How can you be different? How can you grow your business if everyone else is saying they are an expert too? The reality is that we are all different and there is more than enough space and potential clients on this planet for everyone. However, if you don't stand out, you will get lost in the 'noise' that every other expert is making.

A very traditional and perhaps one of the best ways to stand out is with your own book. We are not talking about the next great novel here, rather a book related to your expertise as a business owner, or employee, or a problem that you solve. It could be as simple as the key thing that you are asked about most often, or the nuggets of information that you wish everyone knew? This knowledge captured as a book will propel you and/or your business forward in a way that just isn't otherwise possible with other forms of marketing. So, if you would like to stand out from the crowd and be known as a thought leader then this book is for you.

If you are thinking 'Yes, I have always wanted to write a book and have no idea how to do that', then read on. This book will answer that question as well as many others that you didn't even know you were asking. Typically, we don't know what we don't know, so we have tried to capture everything you need to know about not only becoming a best-selling author, but also how and why to use a book to grow your career or business and earn you a lot more money.

This last part, 'how and why to use a book to grow your career or business and earn you a lot more money' is the most important part and is unfortunately the bit most authors miss out. Which is why most authors don't sell many books or make much money. We wrote this book to help you write your own book, and more importantly, to know what to do with your book once you've written it. Without knowing how to use a book, writing it is actually just a waste of time. After all, being recognised as a thought leader or an expert because you have a book is all very nice, but it won't pay the bills or put food on your table.

However, if you combine the 'expert' reputation created by having your own book, along with our tried-and-tested method of using your book as a business booster, now you'll have the kudos and the money to go with it.

> **Without knowing how to use a book, writing it is actually just a waste of time.**

Having helped thousands of business owners to succeed, we know that at the end of reading this book, there are three likely outcomes.

- Outcome 1, you will know how to write a book, have a structure to do so and be able to bring your ideas together in a manuscript and published book. However, you will have decided that this isn't for you and you'd much rather do something else.

- Outcome 2 is similar to outcome one, however, you'll know you can make it happen and you'll overcome your fears so you can write your book and most importantly start using it to make a bigger difference in the world.

- Outcome 3, similar to outcome 2, however, you would like to work with us directly to short-cut the process, learn how to get paid before you even write your book and produce a best-seller that makes a difference in the world whilst also actually making you money.

Some of you will already be reacting to these options either positively or negatively which will tell you a lot about yourself. You might be someone who doesn't like to be told what is likely. You might be someone who thinks that support is a sign of weakness. Whatever is going on for you as you read this book, take note, as you can use all of these reactions both in your writing and in the writing process itself, as our reactions can either propel us forward or keep us stuck - and we would much prefer you to keep progressing.

"Do what works rather than what's popular".

We're big fans of, "Do what works rather than what's popular". You may be thinking, 'Yes, books have been around for a while, however, aren't they old fashioned and everything is about social media nowadays?' Certainly, all forms of marketing are important. However, the longevity of books proves they are here to stay and will always be 'on trend'. More than that, a book can be a more versatile marketing tool than anything else: it can be something you sell to share your knowledge with a wider audience; it can be a platform or stepping stone into a new career or a leg up in your existing one; it can be a passport to new audiences, new opportunities and a status symbol that few others in your profession will ever achieve. There are so many different uses for a book that other forms of print or marketing just can't compete.

Regardless of what else you might do in your marketing or branding, authorship is the clearest indicator of an expert or thought leader, and thus is the most suitable tool to position yourself as a brand in the long term. If you want to achieve expert status quickly and effectively, a book is your quickest and most reliable route, provided you use it effectively. Even with self-publishing, and more people than ever becoming authors, it is still a very small percentage of the population and you will still stand out and be recognised as an expert.

With a book, and the right knowledge of how to use it, you will automatically get new business and clients. You will develop charisma and magnetic attraction. You may even be regularly booked as a 'speaker'. The press will write about you. You can get in touch with VIPs much more easily. You will automatically enjoy a higher status within your social environment and profit from every book you publish. Whilst this might sound like nirvana, you're right to think this isn't possible for every author. In fact, these results occur for very few authors, unfortunately. Yet, if you 'do the right things in the right order' and follow the path we lay out in this book, all of this and more is possible for you just like it has been for us and our clients.

As a book author, you are in the responsible and fortunate position of being able to help your readers and influence them with your thoughts and words. Or you can polarise them and ignite their passions. Books can change lives. They help people make difficult decisions and transmit completely new knowledge and experiences. Books inspire and encourage their own ideas and actions, and even teach their readers entirely new skills. In writing a book you will also learn a lot more about yourself and those around you.

Personally, for us, books have most definitely changed our lives. In addition to being multi-#1 best-selling authors ourselves, we have always been avid readers and continue to use books to grow our skills, our mindset and our aspirations. We know from our own experience and from the clients we have supported to become high-earning best-selling authors, having your own book will change your life and your business in the long term.

Writing a book is on the 'bucket list' for a lot of people. More than eighty-seven per cent of all people would like to write a book at some point in their lives, yet, only a few manage to do so. In fact, of those who start writing a book, ninety-seven percent give up. Most people let themselves get too caught up in their day-to-day business. They spin on the 'hamster wheel' and never take the time to create this valuable business tool for themselves and put it to work.

However, there are many different ways to both write a book and use a book. Many people get this wrong and either never finish their book or think that when they have finished it, they are done. After all of the effort expended to write a book, we want to make sure that you get a good return on your time and energy investment. With our focus on what works rather than what's popular, we want to make sure that you start with the end in mind and know what to focus on at each part of the journey. Knowing what works and, equally importantly, what doesn't work is going to save you a lot of time and effort in the long run!

In the following chapters, we will explain in detail how you can achieve your goals of writing a book for yourself and begin transforming your life and business. If you are in the enviable position of already having started, or perhaps you have even completed a book and it hasn't been anything other than a long and trying process, then perhaps you missed some steps, particularly those required after you have finished writing.

Something most authors never realise is that it's not about the book. Whilst a great achievement in itself, it's what you do with your book when you have it that makes it either an unparalleled marketing tool, or simply an ego boost that does nothing for your business. This book will help you understand the difference so you can get properly rewarded for all the hard work you'll put into writing your own book.

> **Something most authors never realise is that it's not about the book.**

We hope this book is your passport to a bigger world for yourself so you can take action and become a best-selling author and recognised expert in your domain.

'Taking action, what?!'

You may be thinking, this is a book - I read it, I don't do action. Well, we do, as we know it is action that changes things. Knowledge without action is worthless. Whilst we love reading, we know that reading alone is not enough, so we have written this book with the specific intention to get you into action. For that reason, each of the chapters of this book will move you closer to

> **Knowledge without action is worthless.**

your finished book and the even more important next steps after you become an author.

If you, like us, want to create results, you will be ready to jump straight into action. Great! However, we also know that to be effective, action needs to be preceded by a planning phase otherwise it becomes chaotic and non-focused, which doesn't lead to good results. Plan/Do is a two-step dance we use in all of our businesses and that we teach to our clients. Think of this book as your 'planning' phase, which you need to follow a 'doing' phase of specific actions. Each chapter is written with specific actions or questions designed to give you actions that move you forward to the next step of your author journey. Step by step, we intend to move you from whatever point you are at right now, to becoming a best-selling author, and then to using your book to earn you significant amounts of money. It all starts here with the following questions...

What has made you interested in writing a book?

What would life look/sound/feel/taste like now that you have written a book?

What are all the good things that will come from being an author?

What are your fears or concerns about being an author?

These questions have been specifically chosen to connect you to the 'success' that being an author will provide, as well as to the fears and obstacles that might stop you. We know that the reason most people don't start or finish writing a book is because they get in their own way, so let's start addressing this right away so you can move forward and create your unfair advantage over your competitors.

CHAPTER 1

Where does a book fit into your Business or Career?

In the end we all become stories
- Margaret Atwood

Reading is well established as an important activity. It reduces stress, improves knowledge, increases vocabulary, improves memory and focus and is well studied as one of the greatest predictors for success in most exams. Many of the world's most successful people are avid readers. So, if you, like us, are looking for shortcuts to success, reading and modelling other people's success is probably something you will no doubt be familiar with. With reading being so important for success, being an author with your own book to share with others just makes sense.

There are many different types of books and many different uses for them. To be clear, we are not talking about the next great novel here, although many business books written as parables or stories are very well received. Rather we are talking about a book that showcases your expertise and is used as a marketing tool to build your business or career.

We have briefly mentioned that by writing your own book, you may create a new job, a better job, new clients, more clients, a better business, a platform for speaking opportunities, and so much more. And you are probably asking how a book can deliver these results? In this chapter we will be looking at the key ingredients of a business and how a book can enhance these ingredients for success.

Whether you are an employee or a business owner, you are your own business..

Before we do that however, we have to establish a couple of things so you understand where we are coming from. Firstly, we need you to understand that whether you are an employee or a business owner, you are your business. And secondly, a business is composed of just three things.

Many expert or service-based businesses are so connected with helping people, they forget they're running a business and it can therefore feel like it's a vocation, a job or worse yet, be seen as a hobby. Similarly, as an employee, you can be focused on your 'job' and forget that you are in the business of providing your skills and expertise in exchange for your salary.

Many times, organisations refer to their employees as their greatest assets and yet, their employees or even business owners are not connected with this themselves.

If you aren't connected with the 'value' you provide to a business, then chances are it has been a while since you had a promotion or took on a new or different role. It's possible you may have lost your identity within your business and forgotten that you are separate from it. If you look at successful employees and successful entrepreneurs, they all have a brand, they stand in their expertise and understand that this has value.

Perhaps ask yourself:

Are you thinking like a business owner or as someone getting paid for using his/her skills? If you are a business owner, are you acting like it?

Once you start embracing the idea that you are your business, how you approach life will start to change. This may be liberating, or you may have some concerns. You may be thinking that you don't have any 'business' skills despite having successfully got to wherever you are right now. Being conscious of these business skills will allow you to be even more successful going forward, and we will touch on some of these throughout this book. Of course, without this book being many hundreds of pages longer than it already is, we can't possibly cover all of them in enough detail here. However, if you would like to know more about how to successfully grow a business from £0-£250,000, please check out, 'Grow Your Heart Centred Business: From Passion to Profit' by Chris and Karene Lambert-Gorwyn.

A BUSINESS IS THREE THINGS

Whether you have a product business or a service business, all businesses have three ingredients they need to survive.

1. Marketing
2. Sales
3. Delivery

Similarly, you, as a business, will also need these three things and you will also need to be clear where your book fits into these. Not recognising that a business is three things, or merging these three things together, is usually where people get into difficulty and struggle to succeed.

For example, if you are trying to sell when you should be marketing, you will come across as pushy. We've all experienced those people out networking (a marketing activity) and all they can talk about is how you should buy whatever they are selling (clearly sales - although let's be

A business
is just

3 things:

Marketing

Sales

Delivery

honest, this is definitely not good sales). It doesn't feel good right?

At our Business Trainings, we even have a description for these types of people - they come across as if they have "Money Breath!" This means they are desperate to sell something and make money. This is not a great attribute and it won't build your business! If you are networking, you should be marketing not selling. If you find yourself selling when you should be marketing, STOP IT! Selling whilst marketing will repel clients rather than attract them, which is why marketing, sales and delivery are separate rather than merged activities.

> **Selling whilst marketing will repel clients rather than attract them.**

In your book, for example, if you spend most of your time talking about how great you are and what working with you might look like, rather than sharing useful information that will move people forward, your readers will be put off and think you have just created a sales pamphlet.

If you are marketing when you should be selling, you will never get around to asking for the money because you'll still be talking about how great your services are. This means you'll struggle to sell anything and you won't get paid. For example, if someone has come to see you for a consultation, it means they want to solve a problem or change something. This will usually require them to buy a product or service, so you have to allow them the chance to pay you money otherwise they can't get the help or service they want and need. Learning how to sell effectively is a core business skill.

In your book, if you don't provide next steps, a way to contact you, or an option for people to accelerate their journey by working with you directly, you are doing them a disservice.

If you deliver your product or services when you should be selling, you will probably feel like you're doing a lot of work for free...because you are! If you are not selling, you are not getting paid. This can lead to resentment, burn out, or just plain not earning money for all the effort that you are putting in.

In your book, we want you to be 'delivering', as you want to be 'giving' away your expertise for the price of the book, knowing that there are some people who could never afford the investment of time and/or money to work with you directly. It is therefore key that you provide enough useful content for your readers to be able to take action and hopefully create a real solution to their problems. We are certainly aiming for that with this book! We know that if you follow the systems we give you, along with working on your mindset through the questions and guidance we'll provide, you will become a successful author and either want to work with us further, or happily recommend us to other people because our book and our systems deliver. This means that in this situation, focusing on 'delivery' is actually how we effectively market ourselves.

> The vision of our multiple businesses is, "Grow your business, grow yourself".

When you understand the three areas of business better and develop your skills in each of them, you will be far more powerful in growing your business, which in many cases will also mean that you will be growing yourself. This is why the vision of our multiple businesses is, "Grow your business, grow yourself"

Learning to keep these three key business ingredients separate and using them at the right time will also ensure you are as effective as possible in every situation. We're going to briefly describe each of the business areas here so you have a basic understanding because this is key for both positioning your book and also for what type of content you might want to include in your book.

MARKETING

Marketing is all about getting more clients through your door. Or, as we like to define it, marketing is how you attract more of your ideal clients. Your ideal clients are those

> Marketing is how you attract more of your ideal clients.

ones you really want to work with. The ones who get good results from your services, that you enjoy spending time with, and who happily pay you whatever you ask. More of these types of clients is usually a good thing for any business!

Marketing can be online or offline and is where most business owners get confused, wasting a lot of time and money. It is also one of the key areas of business to focus on because if you don't have enough clients, you don't really have a business.

The confusion in marketing is usually as a result of merging marketing with sales and/or delivery. Marketing is a very discrete filtering process to help you stand out from your competition, and to allow your potential clients to understand what solutions you might be able to offer them. At this point there should be no mention of price, or details of how you do what you do, such as specific tools or techniques. These are sales details and you don't have permission to talk about this yet as you are still marketing.

During marketing you need to establish whether someone is curious to find out more. If they are curious and want to understand more details, great. However, don't give them the details in this conversation otherwise you are merging sales into a marketing conversation. Instead, organise a separate and longer conversation where you can really get to understand what is going on for them and they can get to understand how you work. This is how you move from marketing into sales.

For a book, marketing comes in various forms. Your book itself can be a strategic marketing tool, providing credibility and sharing your expertise with your ideal clients. Your book could be something that you give out to potential clients who, either in reading it or just having it, want to know more about you or to work with you directly. From this initial interest, you can then move them into a sales conversation.

Heart Centred Sales is all about service.

SALES

Heart Centred Sales is all about service. How are you serving your clients and what problems are you solving for them in return for them investing their time and money to work with you? Sales is key in business because you make money when you sell something. Sales is also one area that most people hate or avoid, when in reality it is central to any successful business.

Typically, people have a negative reaction to sales because far too often it is done badly or in the wrong order...remember we mentioned doing the right things in the right order? It is critical that you have permission to sell. You get permission during marketing to allow you to transition to sales. But remember, these are separate activities. Without having permission to sell, you will come across as pushy or negatively salesy, neither of which is a great experience for anyone (think the stereotypical dodgy used car salesman).

Sales is all about finding out what your potential client wants/needs and then working out whether or not you are the best person to support them. We refer to Heart Centred Sales as the discovery of a match. If you are not a match, you don't work together. If you are a match, then you do. The sales conversation is where you discover if you are a match or not. This could take place in an official consultation, or discovery session, or any form of more detailed conversation taking place with a potential client in person, on the phone or online where you have agreed to speak to explore working together.

For a book, there is of course the initial sale. A lot of people think that they will make money from these sales, and, yes, you will make some. However, it is most definitely less than you think!

If you publish and market conventionally with a big publishing house, you are likely to be paid 50p to £1.20 per book sold. If you Self Publish, you can make more, although unfortunately it will still not be enough to change your life: from £1.50

to perhaps £13.00 per book sold. Without the support of a marketing department from a publishing house, most people will only sell less than 500 books, which is probably only a few thousand pounds in income from direct book sales.

The thing most authors never realise is that the biggest revenue from books rarely comes from books sales itself. Instead, it is how you use your book and what offers you provide your readers. For example, you could have a special offer in your book that allows them to talk to you or your team directly about additional support? Or they could purchase something else at an exclusive discounted rate? Perhaps you facilitate this by calling everyone who buys your book and starting a conversation? Or allowing them to join a group of other readers who may be able to support each other with their experiences? Or by sending them to an online landing page with some clear next steps? As your reader has already bought your book, they are much more likely to buy something else from you because they clearly have some sort of interest in the problems that you solve. This is where you would move further into delivery.

DELIVERY

Delivery is all about fulfilling what you have sold. Whatever your expertise, delivery is when you perform whatever it is you do for your clients. This can be directly client facing, or could be through activities required to support a person or business such as admin, compliance, or other professional services.

In most instances, this will be the content of your book. Your expertise is captured on the page for your ideal clients to learn from, apply to their lives or businesses and, ultimately, to change and grow in some way as a result of what they have read. By helping your readers increase their knowledge and see things from a different perspective, they can't help but change and progress in some way.

With a basic understanding of each of these three areas of business, you will be able to use them more effectively in your client journey and your book. Being more effective means adding more value to your clients and readers. Adding more value will result in increased revenue. For example, perhaps you ask for referrals (marketing) from a reader (delivery). You follow up with the referral you are given (marketing) and perhaps offer some initial free advice (delivery). If they are curious to learn more, you schedule a consultation (sales) to explore working together. If you are a match (sales), you ask for and receive payment and schedule your first session in the diary (delivery).

> **Regardless of where you are in your career or your business, clarity is key.**

Regardless of where you are in your career or your business, clarity is key. Without understanding the distinction of these separate business areas, you are likely to end up in a muddle: stuck trying to convince people to work with you and hating sales; giving away your time for free; not growing your business; or worst yet, having to give up your business or dreams because you can't make it work.

Work out whether you are making use of the three key areas of business and whether you are keeping them separate. If you are great, if not, work out what you are perhaps combining to your detriment and change it. After all, you are not a tree so you can move and change how you do things. Still not quite sure? That's ok, in the next chapter we are going to explore when and how you should focus on each of these areas in your book to be more successful.

CHAPTER 2

It's not about the book!
Your Book as a Marketing Tool

There is more treasure in books than in all the
pirate's loot on Treasure Island - Walt Disney

Before we delve into why books are so great for marketing,
we need to understand what marketing is and how come
it is such a focus for people and businesses. This chapter
will provide you with a clearer understanding of marketing,
how to identify your ideal client and what all of this means
for your book.

The biggest challenge most businesses
face is getting enough clients
walking through their door. If
you don't have enough clients,
all other aspects of the business
will struggle because there's
simply not enough people or
money flowing into your business.
Having spent many years presenting

**The biggest
challenge most
businesses face is
getting enough clients
walking through
their door.**

---

at business and financial conferences around the world, whenever we ask people if they would like a long line of new clients waiting for them when they get back to work, the response is always overwhelmingly, "Yes!"

However, to challenge that belief slightly, most businesses couldn't actually handle a long line of new clients waiting to work with them. They simply don't have the capacity or the business systems to handle a massive influx of new clients. It might sound strange but over-demand is actually just as damaging as under-demand and can lead to just as many stresses and challenges. The most common thing people say they want when they start working with us is that they want to be fully booked with clients. However, a few months later, when we get them fully booked, the most common thing we hear is, "I wish I had more time and some gaps in my diary!"

So, rather than blindly wanting more clients, it's important to get clear on how many you really want and need, and more importantly, how you're going to serve them when they arrive.

The thing is though, there is an underlying fear of rejection that maintains the reality for most business owners of not having enough clients. This fear leads us to think we need huge numbers of clients because if we have lots of clients, clearly we are not being rejected. Unfortunately, this fear is often perpetuated by a lot of educators irresponsibly embedding the belief that, "If you are good enough, people will come".

Rest assured this is not the case! Being good at what you do is of course part of any successful business. But your potential clients have no idea if you're good or not and won't find out until they start working with you. It's all down to your marketing skills, not your professional skills that will determine whether or not you have enough new clients walking through your door. This is why the belief of "If you're good enough, people will come" is so damaging, because it means most experts go out and keep getting more and more education and skills in their expertise to become a better practitioner/expert, rather than just learning how to effectively market themselves. Again, the key is to recognise you are in business and therefore need to focus on learning how to better do business activities such as marketing.

Conventional wisdom in marketing and getting more clients is that to reach more people, you have to go online. Put your message in front of thousands of people online and some are bound to want to work with you right?

Sadly, no. If it were really that easy, every person with a website or on social media would be a millionaire. The hard truth is that if you can't get clients in your local area through person-to-person interaction, that is, talking to people, it's highly unlikely that your marketing message is going to be effective when put online in front of thousands.

Until you have perfected your marketing message and know how to market effectively in person, online marketing will just create a more expensive challenge.

Yet the online world is more alluring than going out and speaking to people, because real life people could say "No". Being told 'no' in person will trigger fear of rejection. Far safer to go online instead and hide behind a computer screen. However, the reality is, if you don't get clients from your online marketing, you are actually being rejected by thousands of people at a time - you just don't notice it because it's not as if everyone posts a "No thank you" message. Also, even if it doesn't seem like it, the competition online from other professionals is far greater than that in your local area. Suddenly, you are competing on a global scale with other experts who are more qualified, willing to work for less money and who are probably younger and better looking as well!

Now, this is not to say that the online world doesn't work for marketing. Of course it does and, if used well, can be massively effective at getting you new clients. However, always remember, it is about doing the right things in the right order. Until you have perfected your marketing message and know how to market effectively in person, online marketing will just create a more expensive challenge.

Simone from Brighton is a great example of how this might show up. With a lifetime of accumulated skills and qualifications, she had no business, no direction and no paying clients. However, she had created a great website to hide behind that she spent hours tweaking and refining and she still had no paying clients. A great website is one thing, however, if there's no traffic (people) going to your website, tweaking the content on the website to make it prettier is like cutting the grass in a ghost town. This is the point that Simone joined our award winning Passion to Profit Mentorship Programme. Unfortunately, she then spent the first 6 months of it ignoring what we taught her and continuing hiding behind her website, hoping it would all work out. When she finally accepted that this wasn't working and started implementing our systems, she started doing the right things in the right order. For her, at the stage of business she was at, this was offline person-to-person marketing. Once she started this, the results started to come in. 18 months later Simone had as many clients as she wanted, all paying more than £1,000 to work with her. She works only during school hours, so she can spend time being a mum and has been able to leave her part-time job as a teacher which she previously needed to pay the bills.

As she puts it, she now has "bundles of self-worth and loves living life full out!"

MARKETING IS A FILTER NOT A NET

Marketing and, more specifically, Attraction Marketing is about having more of your ideal clients walking through your door. If you don't have enough clients, this is where you need to focus your efforts.

If you are lacking clients, you may, like most people, be trying to market to anyone and everyone in the hope that it delivers clients. Most people think of marketing as a net to catch customers. This is not a very collaborative, nor a very useful metaphor for either the business or the customer. Any business casting a 'net' appears to be indiscriminately trying to snare anyone who comes their way. From a customer's perspective, the net analogy does not feel great because it implies that they are merely fish or unimportant individuals who have no choice other than to be dragged into the business and parted from their money.

Heart Centred Business and Attraction Marketing turns this typical net view of marketing on its head. Instead of marketing being a net that takes in anyone it can catch, we view marketing as a filter. As there are more than 7 billion people living on this Earth, marketing is the filter a business uses to find its perfect customers who will most appreciate and benefit from its services. This is why it's called Attraction Marketing.

Attraction Marketing does exactly what it says on the tin and attracts ideal clients, actively filtering out everyone else who might not be appropriate. This means being very specific about who you want to work with, something that many business owners are resistant to doing. We admit, we were also very resistant when we first learnt this approach.

Most businesses think by marketing to everyone, they will generate a high demand for their products and services. Yet, in reality, it's the complete opposite. It might seem counter-intuitive, but the more specific you are in your marketing, the more clients you will attract. Market to everyone, you'll end up attracting no one! This is because the more general the marketing message, the less specialised your services appear, and people can't see themselves in your solution.

In business, you can either be seen as a specialist or a generalist. Both have their place in this world and yet we would always recommend your business be positioned and seen as an expert or specialised service. How come? Very simply, specialists make more money and help more people.

Think of it this way... If you had a severe headache that had lasted for several weeks and all the normal pain killers aren't working, would you rather visit your local GP (Family Doctor) or a Brain Surgeon?

It's the Brain Surgeon every time isn't it, even if you desperately hope you don't need brain surgery?! Why is this? A GP is a generalist, whereas a brain surgeon is a specialist. When we have big enough issues or challenges, we want a specialist because they will be better positioned to be able to help us.

Now who would you pay more money to see, the GP or the brain surgeon?

Again, it's the brain surgeon every time isn't it?!

We all naturally expect to pay more to see a specialist and if we have a big enough problem, we'll happily pay whatever is needed to get a solution. This is why any business will be more successful if it positions itself as a specialist rather than a generalist in its marketing. Of course, a specialist service is not going to be for everyone, so marketing in this way acts as a filter and actively turns off people who do not have the problems that your business solves. Simultaneously it will also attract people who need and want your specialised services.

In order to be seen as a specialist rather than a generalist, we have to communicate effectively who we are best suited to work with and what particular problem we specialise in solving. A lot of businesses try to be everything to everyone. This is why they struggle. And even if this type of marketing did work and they could appeal to every person on this planet, remember there are over 7 billion of us! Most businesses would collapse if all 7 billion people suddenly appeared asking to buy their services. Let's face it, even one hundred new clients turning up on the same day, or even within the same week, it would be a challenge for most small businesses because they simply do not have the capacity to handle that number of new clients.

And if you're still harbouring any concerns about narrowing down your niche or focusing on a smaller target group of potential clients, remember the 7 billion humans? Even if what you do will only appeal to one in a million people, that still means you have over 7000 potential clients who will love what you do. 7000 clients is more than enough for most businesses!

As we've mentioned before, we are big fans of doing the right things in the right order and being as efficient as possible with our time. We're sure that you, like us, have many other things you could be doing with your time. Getting a consistent flow of new clients into your business from a minimal outlay of time and effort would make things a lot easier, right?

In this chapter on Attraction Marketing, we are going to get clear on what you need for an effective marketing filter, which is particularly pertinent to writing a book as you want to both be seen as an expert and make your book relevant to the right people. To do that we need to understand 2 things:

1. What is needed for marketing to be effective.

2. Your message to market using Person Problem Solution.

We're going to cover these progressively in the following sections of this chapter.

MARKETING IS 2 THINGS

To create an effective marketing filter, we firstly need to know what is needed for marketing to be effective. Very simply, marketing needs two components. Achieve these two components and your marketing has been successful and you can now progress into sales. Fail to get either of these two components and your marketing just won't work and you won't have anyone to move into sales conversations. These two components are:

1. Attention
2. Curiosity

Component 1 of successful marketing is getting attention. If you don't break through the everyday noise that surrounds us nowadays and get someone's attention, then how will they know your business exists?

Attention can be gained in both positive and negative ways, and we've all experienced both.

For example, if you're standing on a crowded platform and someone stands on a box and starts shouting, 'Listen to me!', they probably have got your attention. What they say next though determines whether it is a positive or a negative experience for you.

If they say, 'Look out, there's a fire over there! Come this way!', you'd probably be pretty glad they got your attention. If they instead started swearing, shouting abuse, or telling you, "The Lord is your saviour!" you'd probably just dismiss them..

A business needs to break through the noise in the marketplace to get people's attention, but it doesn't always have to shout. The more specific the message you have, the more your marketing will stand out to certain people. This means if you are an early stage business and have a low budget, it's ok as you don't need to produce an all-singing, all-dancing, slick marketing campaign. And if you are already a well-established business with an online presence, using a more specific message will mean your marketing budget will be spent more wisely.

The most effective way of getting attention is to speak directly to other human beings.

The most effective way of getting attention is to speak directly to other human beings. And the easiest, simplest and most cost-effective way to do this is to connect with your local community. Become part of your local community and serve them. By being ultra-specific with your marketing message, you get the reputation of being an expert. This reputation, then further spreads the word about what you do, so you will reach more people.

This is the same for your book. Your title, colours of the cover etc will all work toward getting people's attention. Simply having your own book will allow you to stand out as an expert.

Will this specificity get everyone's attention? Of course not, and that's a good thing! Remember, most businesses do not have the capacity to work with hundreds of people, so we need to filter out a LOT of people to find the ones we can help.

Once we have people's attention, we now need to generate curiosity.

Curiosity is essential to move from marketing into heart centred sales. Without curiosity, people are not ready for a sales conversation because they have no interest in buying. Think of the situation in a shop when you are just looking and the salesperson tries to convince you to buy whatever you glance at. It's irritating and a complete turn off because you're not at that stage yet. This is the mistake many people make around sales. They get people's attention and without waiting for curiosity, they move straight into sales. This means they end up trying to force or convince people to buy their services. This is not heart centred sales!

If curiosity is generated, it means the other person is ready to explore whether or not the product or service is right for them. This means marketing has been successful. It is now appropriate to move into a sales conversation.

How do we gauge curiosity?

If you get people's attention in the right way, it will generate curiosity in people who your services are relevant for. Of course, if your services are not relevant to someone, it is unlikely to elicit curiosity, so the filter works. There are many clues to look for that will indicate whether someone is curious to explore more about your services. The most obvious is that they ask for more information. If they haven't asked, they might still be curious, however, you will need to assure yourself in a different way. It might be that you ask them, "Would you be curious to know more?"

Please note, it is very important you use the word 'curious' here instead of the word 'interested'. You can be curious without making a commitment so it is a safe word to use that won't turn people off. The minute you use the word 'interested' there is an implied commitment and we aren't there yet. I know this might not seem like a big deal, however, it really is. The subtlety of the words that you use can be the difference between you making a connection or not, so always pay attention to both your language and the other person's.

If you're speaking to someone in person, other indicators of curiosity could be more subtle, such as an altered body position like leaning in or stepping forward. Paying attention to someone's response will allow you to determine if you have achieved attention and curiosity and is critical to understanding if your marketing has been successful.

In order to effectively get people's attention and generate curiosity, we need to go right back to basics and determine what your business does, so we can start communicating effectively with the people who need your services. Once we have created the right message to get the attention and curiosity of your clients, we can use this to work out how to market your book and also where your book needs to be to get into the hands of your ideal customers.

Some questions you might want to consider at this point are:

- What do you currently do to attract attention? What else could you do?
- What do you currently do to gauge curiosity? What else could you do?
- When thinking about your upcoming book, consider how you will get people's attention and generate

curiosity in order to help the right people move forward.

If you can't yet answer these questions, read on.

PERSON, PROBLEM, SOLUTION

Most businesses struggle to articulate what they do, so when it comes to a book that highlights your expertise, this may also be a struggle. This might seem strange but just think about it for a moment...

How many businesses or people do you know that can succinctly articulate the exact type of person they work with and the perfect problem that they are able to provide a solution for?

And do it in less than 20 seconds?

Not many, right? And often when the problem or solution is described, it uses technical jargon only familiar to people trained in that area.

To give you an example, Chris trained and worked as an Osteopath for nearly 20 years. Many Osteopaths (as well as Chiropractors, Physiotherapists and all manner of other practitioners) could describe what they do by saying something along the lines of 'We manipulate the musculoskeletal structure to restore the correct neurological and vascular balance to the body.'

Did you understand that, because a lot of people wouldn't?! Whilst technically correct, a statement like this completely alienates a lot of people because it uses technical jargon and doesn't tell us what problems these Osteopaths or any other practitioners solve or who they work with. If a business description cannot be understood by a 10-year-old child, it doesn't work and is too complex.

If a business description cannot be understood by a 10-year-old child, it doesn't work and is too complex.

If we re-wrote the exact same statement above in a different way, it could say 'We help people in pain to stand up straight, so they look and feel better.' This is saying the same thing but in terms anyone can understand. The more people who understand what you do, the better chance you have of getting more clients walking through your door.

Now, the simplified description we gave of what an Osteopath/Chiropractor/Physiotherapist etc could say is an improvement on the first statement. Yet it is still positioning the business as a generalist rather than a specialist service. Yes, it's slightly specific because it mentions that they work with people in pain, yet it is still in GP/Family Doctor territory rather than Brain Surgeon levels of perceived specialism and expertise.

Something to note, the simplified description doesn't include anything about the practitioner's expertise or how they get clients results. There is nothing about 'how' Osteopaths get their clients better. This is a good thing! Discussion about manipulation, mobilisation, soft tissue massage or any other technique is completely irrelevant to potential clients. Of course, most business owners are very proud of their skills and techniques and may have spent many years building up their expertise. Of course they want to show off their knowledge and skill set and they assume everyone is as interested in their skills as they are.

The reality is somewhat different! We're going to be direct here...

"No one cares what you do, until they know what you can do for them!"

Until we know what's in it for us, we just don't pay attention to things. This sounds harsh, yet it's the simple reality that, as humans, we filter out most of the things around us to allow us to focus on what we perceive as important. If something doesn't appear immediately relevant to us, it gets lost in the background noise. No matter how proud we are of them, our titles, qualifications, techniques, skills etc all fall under the category of irrelevant to most people because they don't understand how it relates to them. Therefore, there is no benefit to saying any of it in your marketing if you want to be effective! All of this detail is for clients once they have purchased your services, not before. You could include some of it in the content of your book if it is fundamentally useful for people to understand, however, it definitely doesn't need to feature on the front cover or in any of your marketing.

One further thing to consider is your clients really don't care 'how' you get them results. They just want results - period! In Chris' clinic, he specialised in working with women in their 50's with over 10 years of unresolved low back pain. He was known by his clients as the go-to guy in London to 'fix' long-term back pain. The thing is though, none of his clients cared or even knew that he was an Osteopath. They didn't care what techniques he used, or what courses or training he had done - they just wanted to get out of pain. He could have waved feathers around or done a rain dance and they wouldn't have batted an eyelid - as long as they got results.

So, if we don't say our titles or anything about how we do what we do, then what do we say when we're marketing?!

Your book will face this exact same challenge. We can help you become a best-selling author, which of course will make you feel like you are very impressive and will be great for your ego, however, let's face it, it won't make much difference to anyone else - except perhaps your mum! That best-seller title is only relevant to other people when they think you can help them with their specific problems. As we've said before, it's what you do with your best-selling book that counts, and this comes down to marketing.

Think about what your potential clients/readers need to hear in order to decide whether or not to work with you. Primarily, they just want the headline information about what outcome you get for your clients. For example, when we are asked what we do, we simply say, This obviously will appeal to some people and not to others, so it acts as 'We're on a mission to create 1000 heart centred millionaires.' a filter. It deliberately doesn't say anything about what we do, who we are, or anything about our multiple companies and various services we offer. It just focuses on the end result. For some people this will get their attention and create curiosity. For others it won't.

However, if you don't have such a clear-cut mission or goal in your business, sometimes it's better to give a bit more detail in order to help people get a greater understanding.

Again, focus on what will cut through the noise and give your potential clients the information they need. We need to focus on saying who you work with and what problems you solve for these people. Distilling this down to basics, it comes down to:

> **'We're on a mission to create 1000 heart centred millionaires.'**

Person
Problem

Solution

Describe your ideal client (PERSON), the challenges they usually come to you with (PROBLEM), and finally the ultimate outcomes they get from working with you (SOLUTION).

To give you some examples of what we've personally used successfully in some of our businesses...

In Heart Centred Business, our business training company...

'We typically work with women in their 40's who run a 6-figure business and are frustrated they're still working too many hours for too little profit. We grow their business from 6 to 7 figures, so they can take home more money and start enjoying life outside work again.'

In Chris's clinic, he used to say...

'I typically work with women aged 45-55 who own their own business and have struggled with over 10 years of unresolved low back pain. I get them out of pain permanently and create a long-term solution whilst helping them step up in their life and business in ways they haven't been able to for years.'

In our Property Investment Company, we say...

'We help families who can't afford to buy their own home by providing high-quality rented accommodation in commutable locations across the country.'

In HCB Publishing we say...

'We work with experts who feel like they are the worlds best kept secret. We help them become recognised as a thought leader so they create more success and earn more money.'

Now, in each of these businesses we are describing our ideal clients. Why is this so important? Well, if marketing is a filter, let's filter for the clients you want, rather than just any old client!

The challenge most business owners face though is deciding who is their ideal client.

'I can help everybody' is the classic resistance we hear when we suggest becoming this specific, and Chris was no different when he started with this in his clinic. Remember, there are 7 billion+ humans out there. Yes, you might have the ability to help everyone, but you most definitely do not have the capacity to help everyone.

Similarly, you might be thinking you need multiple versions of this Person, Problem, Solution depending on who you're talking to...?

No, you don't. If you change your marketing message depending on your audience, you are no longer a specialist and are just a generalist trying to appeal to everyone.

Roy, for example, a client of ours who typically works with women in the corporate world to help them break through the glass ceiling and reach board level positions, would still say this to a room of men. Why, because although he markets to women, it doesn't mean he only works with women. He would also work with men if they were a match to work together. However, because his ideal clients are women, that is who he markets for and why he uses the words 'I typically work with women..." He doesn't say, "I exclusively work with women..."

Some men hearing Roy's marketing message want the outcome he describes for themselves and so ask for a further conversation - they're curious. Other men, hearing that he works with women will be completely turned off and are therefore not a match to work with him. This is the benefit of using marketing as a filter. Roy ends up being seen as a specialist, having sales conversations with people who are already predisposed to working with him, rather than trying to convince everyone and ending up being a generalist working with no one.

We know that you will be tempted to do things differently and to try it your way. Chris certainly did this for a while, and guess what, it works best when you just follow the system of what works rather than trying to reinvent the wheel. We also know you probably are having a 'Yes, but...' moment so by all means go ahead and try if you must, however, know that you will get the best results when you follow the system.

If you're having a blank on who your ideal clients are, here are 3 questions to help you define them. Even if you are an employee, you will have stakeholders, perhaps internal clients, or your organisation will have clients and which of those are your ideal will become clear. Once you know your ideal client, you can create your own Person, Problem, Solution marketing statement and start attracting more of them into your business.

Question 1.

Out of all the clients you've ever worked with, who has gotten the best results?

This would be someone who thinks you can walk on water because you have made such a difference to them.

Question 2.

Out of all the clients you've ever worked with, who have you most enjoyed working with?

This person or group of people are such fun to work with, you actively look forward to them showing up and would happily work with them for free.

Question 3.

Out of all the clients you've ever worked with, who paid the best?

Now we know this is deliberately clunky English, however, it refers to several different components:

- Which client has paid you the most in one transaction?
- Which client has paid you the most over time?

- Which client has told you that you're too cheap and should be charging more?

Try answering these questions with a specific person in mind, if possible; or at the very least, a small number of people. Once you have an answer to each question, go through the answers and look for similarities that appear in all 3 answers. This will then help you create a picture of your ideal client: someone who gets good results from what you do, is fun to work with, and who happily pays you a lot of money!

For example, it could be that the answers to these 3 questions are all women; or all men; or they're all in their 20's; or 40's; or all play tennis; or all come from a particular networking group; or all suffer from headaches; or all need confidence coaching etc.

Once you know the characteristics, you can create a marketing statement that lists Person, Problem, Solution for your ideal client. Having this clarity and being able to say this in response to the question, 'What do you do?' will dramatically increase the chances of having more of your ideal clients walk through your door.

Now, let me just check...are you thinking, 'Surely getting more clients can't be this simple?! I just stop telling people my title or qualification, stop talking about skills and techniques and simply describe my ideal client, the problems they have and the solution I provide, and I will get lots more clients?'

Yes, it really is that simple.

When we first started using Person, Problem, Solution in Chris' clinic business, Chris had already been in the practitioner world for nearly 15 years. He was very good at what he did, yet only earning around £2000 a month and struggling to get new clients. Two weeks after starting to use Person, Problem, Solution as a marketing message, he had earned £4000. He had doubled his client numbers and therefore his income in just two weeks by simply changing his marketing message!

Now we talked about wanting you to take action and now is a great time to move from planning and into doing. At this point you may also come up with excuses as to how now isn't the right time and that's ok too, just take note of where you are and what you are prepared to do or not to do.

Whenever you do choose to move into action, answer the 3 questions above to determine your ideal client. From these answers create your Person, Problem, Solution marketing message. This will really help when it comes to getting specific about your book and you might now pause here, however, if you are ready to push your comfort zone there are some additional actions you can take. Get on the phone (yes, the phone, not text,

Be brave, pick up the phone and connect with a human.

social media or smoke signals) and share your new message with at least 10 people this week and ask for their opinion.

We specifically suggest using the phone because it will be quicker, although doing it in-person will have the same result as it needs to be a conversation. This conversation and the real-time sharing will allow you to test out your message and experience how it lands. You will therefore be able to refine your message through experience and feedback, as well as spreading the word to your friends and family about what you do in your business so they can start making referrals to you. If you do this via messages or social media you won't get the same kind of feedback, so Be brave, pick up the phone and connect with a human.

Now you might be a bigger business and you can see how you apply this to yourself as an individual. However, how does this apply to the wider business/practice/other services you offer?

The simple answer is, it applies in much the same way. However, you do it at a practice/business level and your employees all have their own individual marketing messages that fit within the company message. Whether, as the business owner, you describe what your business does, or what you do personally, will depend on what outcome you are after. If you want to grow the business, describe the business. If you want clients for a particular person or area within the business, then describe that.

If you have a group of different skill sets as a business, you might be more focused on your values or approach rather than the individual professions. As an example, Marcus, who has a business with revenues of approx £1M pa, is focused on 3 areas of wellness: Body, Mind, Nutrition to cover the various different things his business covers.

Karene used to work for a very successful multinational consultancy. To describe what they did, she would say, 'We typically worked with FTSE 100 companies struggling with profitability. We supported them in delivering increased shareholder value with an engaged workforce.' There is a clear person, or in this case, organisation. A clear problem: their struggle with profitability. And a solution: increased shareholder value whilst caring for their people. The HOW is irrelevant as this marketing message will either attract attention and create curiosity or it won't.

Because getting more clients is such a key challenge for most businesses, it is very hard to resist the temptation to try everything at once. This is why focusing on a book and targeting it specifically to the wants and needs of your ideal clients, using the ideas in this chapter will give you an advantage over most people. Being clear on your marketing message will allow you to achieve success levels that others can't because they lack this focus and are still trying to be all things to all people.

CHAPTER 3

All the reasons
I can't write a book

The scariest Moment is always just
before you start - Stephen King

At this point we should acknowledge the elephant in the room. For some of us, let's face it, it's not just one elephant, it's an entire herd! When it comes to writing a book, we have a LOT of objections and fears that stop us even starting. No matter how excited or passionate we might be to write our own book, when it comes to actually getting started, those reasons we tell ourselves, or worse yet, that other people have told us, stop us dead in our tracks. Reasons such as, 'I'm not good enough', 'no one will read it anyway so what's the point?', 'I'm dyslexic' and so on ad infinitum.

To help you see these reasons as the self-imposed blocks they actually are, we're going to lay them all out here so that you can acknowledge whatever is going on in your head, move past it and decide with clarity, whether writing a book is the best thing for you and your business, or not.

The right mindset enables you to take action and use the knowledge you have. The reverse is also true, the wrong mindset prevents you from taking action or effectively using the knowledge you have.

The right mindset enables you to take action and use the knowledge you have.

For example, why do men get lost more often than women? One reason could be that men often have a mindset that says it's not manly to ask for directions or look at a map. Women, whilst often more hesitant with their sense of direction, and perhaps because of this, are more willing to ask for directions meaning they are far less likely to get lost along the way. Obviously this does not apply to all men or all women, however, it is common enough to have become a stereotype. Whilst we might not like stereotypes, fundamentally they are always based on something.

This is a great example of a self-sabotaging mindset and many of us do this sort of thing in our business and finances without even realising. Chris will readily admit, along with not asking for directions when he'd get lost driving, that he was also guilty of not asking for directions when he was lost in my business or finances. It took him a long time of winding further and further into debt before his daughter was born and he faced the reality that the discomfort of asking for help was far less than the discomfort of staying lost! His bank balance, and Karene, are definitely happier now he's moved past that particular self-sabotaging mindset.

To support you in upgrading your mindset so it works for you rather than against you, we have a couple of approaches....

We'll share lots of stories from our clients to help you realise, if they can do it, so can you.

We will share our own challenges and failures so you can see how we overcame them and how you could do this in your own life or business.

We'll also explore and help you identify where exactly your mindset might be holding you back. Awareness after all, is the first step to changing these beliefs.

And finally, here and throughout this book, we'll also share tools, strategies, questions and actions that will help you progressively move out of self-sabotage and into whatever level of success you dream of.

Unfortunately for many people, a lack of knowledge or a limited mindset will have already descended into doubt and disbelief that writing a book or being successful might be possible. This is exactly the reason why, so few people ever write their own book, or build a multi-million pound business. The doubts, the disbelief and the lack of knowledge all get in the way and stop us taking action. Which leads to a self-fulfilling prophecy of negativity....thinking we can't succeed, stops us trying to succeed, so we of course don't succeed and then have clear evidence to reinforce our belief that success isn't possible for us. It's time to reverse that negative spiral and turn it into a positive action-based belief system that's reinforced by increasing evidence of success. And it starts with exploring those thoughts and feelings that seem rational and reasonable and yet are actually your very worst enemy!

Remember, as Henry Ford suggested, "Whether you think you can or think you can't, you are right." Whilst profound, this only scratches the surface of the powerful impact our brains have on our experience of the world and the reality we end up living. When it comes to doing anything, we have an internal mindset or belief pattern that is reflected and revealed in our physical or external reality. By this we mean whatever you think and feel leads to how you act. Your actions will create the results and levels of success you have in life and business. Whilst this might sound simple, it really is how it works. What we think and feel creates our reality.

"Whether you think you can or think you can't, you are right."

Not happy with your life, your finances, your business success? Take the time to examine your thoughts and feelings and we guarantee you'll start to understand why you have the reality you have.

By the way, we do acknowledge that this is not always a comfortable thing to do. In fact, it is rarely comfortable! None of us like feeling that we've 'done wrong'. It's far easier and more comfortable (in the short term) to blame other things, other people, or the circumstances at large for what's not going right in our lives. And yet, avoiding responsibility like this means we give up our power to change our circumstances because we stay in 'victim' mode and remain at the mercy of external factors.

By taking responsibility for ourselves and exploring how our own thoughts or feelings could be impacting our actions and therefore the results in our lives, it gives us the power to change our reality because we can choose to think, feel and act differently. Whilst this can be daunting, ultimately it's incredibly liberating. For the first time, you'll actually be in control of the direction your life takes and can act with purpose to create the reality you want. Of course, life will still keep on happening to you, as it does to everyone, yet you now have the opportunity to choose how to respond and that gives you the power to chart your own course.

For example, at the time of writing this, for the last two years, the entire world has been experiencing the massive and varying trials of the Covid pandemic. Everyone has been impacted by this and unfortunately it has pushed many people out of business or created significant financial distress.

We are no exception...pre-pandemic our businesses ranged from investment properties, to a chain of fitness facilities, and a business training company based on running in-person events. Through the same 2 years of stress and upheaval that everyone around the world experienced, an awful lot changed for us, both externally, as well as internally in our mindsets. Whilst the pandemic collectively cost us more than £4million in lost income and expenses, and has caused us more sustained stress than perhaps we have ever experienced previously, we've also formed many new friendships and business partnerships. We now run 8 successful companies instead of 4; we've written 6 best-selling books; relocated to live on the beach instead of in the city; and helped hundreds of business owners survive and even thrive during the times when their colleagues were closing their doors.

Was it easy?

Definitely not!

Yet by staying aware of our thoughts and feelings during the pandemic, we have been able to adapt to the circumstances and find opportunities for growth and success. And those books we wrote during the pandemic whilst juggling all of our businesses, home schooling, serving panicking clients, and moving house...have brought in around £500,000 in revenue. Not through book sales by the way, but through direct sales conversations that have happened because of the books.

Of course it would have been far easier to just furlough all our staff, sit back and hope for it all to be over. However, if you create a mindset of 'What if...?' and 'How can I....?' and combine it with a willingness to put in the work, you will quite literally transform your life forever.

When it comes to the mindset of writing your own book, the key question to ask yourself is, "How much do I want this?" By 'this', we don't actually mean having a book. We mean the life, the finances and the business that you want to create because you have a book. This is a very different way of thinking and is something that most authors never seem to understand. Your book is not the end result. It is simply the tool that will make amazing things happen if you use it effectively.

The key question to ask yourself is, "How much do I want this?"

So, with this in mind, it might actually make it less daunting to take on as a project because it is no longer an ego-trip with everything riding on your producing a perfect manuscript. Instead it is about creating a great tool that will make your life goals much more reachable. Your book doesn't have to be perfect because it's not about the book - it's how you use the book once you have written it!

Saying that, we know there could still be a lot of objections and fear in your head that could stop you if left unchecked so let's go through them together now...

I can't write...I'm not good enough...I'm dyslexic...Poor grammar...Bad handwriting...... insert limited belief around your writing ability here...

Quite a few people were "taught" during school that they were supposedly not good enough to write. They got mediocre or even bad grades for their essays. Their teachers or parents gave them scathing and damaging feedback. Comments such as, 'You should leave the writing to others', or, 'You're not good at writing', can have a long lasting negative impact.

Such statements create inner blocks and belief patterns that we carry from childhood into adulthood as internalised judgements that prevent us from believing in ourselves, daring to try new things and realising their full potential.

David happily admits he is a great example of this...

In school, I was not good at writing, but rather was mathematically gifted. This was reinforced by both my grades and by my teacher's feedback. As I grew older, I played to what

I felt and was told were my strengths by either presenting content visually or giving a lecture instead of putting it down in writing. I never once considered that I could write a book - it wasn't that I didn't want to, it was more that it never crossed my mind because my entire identity around writing was that it wasn't my skill set.

Until one day, I heard about how incredibly effective a book of my own would be as a business tool. I may not have thought I was good at writing but what I was good at was building businesses, so anything that would give me an advantage or additional routes to success was appealing. Once I understood how a book could help me achieve my goals, my reservations about my supposed lack of writing talent were blown away. I really wanted to try it out. I love challenges!

In the beginning, writing was extremely exhausting for me and took up a lot of time. It was literally a case of hard work and willpower forcing me to sit at the computer putting the words down one at a time. But shortly after my first publication, I wrote a non-fiction book on 'How to build a successful elite business in the health and sports industry' - in just a few days.

What was the difference? How was that possible? I followed a system. Then we further developed this system so that other people didn't have to feel that writing wasn't their thing and that writing a book was accessible. At the time of writing this, we have helped close to a hundred people not only write a book but use it to support their career or business. We share this system in Chapter 5.

I have no time...books take ages to write...I'm too busy to take this on... ...insert limited belief around time here...

Instead of writing your book the traditional way, you can 'speak' it and record yourself doing it. All you need is the ability to record and play back speech. You can do this with any computer or phone today. You then get your recording transcribed to make a very solid and easily produced rough draft. From this, it can be turned into a finished and professional book manuscript quickly making the production of your book a much shorter process than writing it in the traditional way.

Dyslexic? Bad handwriting? Slow typer? Poor grammar? Told at school you were rubbish at writing? Or super busy, have limited time and concerned that writing a book takes ages? All these can be solved by speaking your book rather than physically writing it. For David, this was a game changer and it has made becoming an author a lot more fun. Rather than trying to overcome his childhood blocks around writing by sheer force of will, he's been able to bypass them entirely by speaking his books into existence. And you know what, having multiple books on his bookshelf with his name on the cover has proved a great way to put to rest his lingering doubts around not being good enough at writing to become an author.

> **I'm not good enough...I don't know what to write...no one will want to read my book... there's already so many books on this subject already...who am I to say I'm an expert and write a book...my teacher/master/guru doesn't have a book and they're much better than me... ...insert limited belief around your expertise here...**

You think you can't write a book because you lack the talent or you're not enough of an expert? Remember, it is not about the book!

The book isn't the end result, it is a tool to connect you to people and help them understand how you could help them. And if you are already serving people with your expertise currently, then you are enough of an expert to write a book.

Remember, it is not about the book!

For some people even calling themselves an expert is a big enough challenge on its own. Seeing themselves as a best-selling author is an entire paradigm shift of mindset that whilst confronting, is exactly why it is such a powerful tool for building your reputation. If you are blown away at the thought of being 'good enough' to have written your own book, that is exactly the thought that everyone else is going to have. You will instantly stand out in their minds, head and shoulders above everyone else in your profession.

This is one of the reasons why a book is such a good tool for building your business or career. But first you have to get out of your own way and realise you actually are good enough at what you do to write a book about it. How do we do this?

Step one is recognising you are an expert to anyone you know more than. We guarantee you know more about your subject matter than your clients, which is why they come to you in the first place, or if you are employed that is why you get paid. Your clients or employer are paying you for your knowledge and expertise so you can help them with whatever challenge they are undergoing. This means that if you wrote your knowledge down, it would be useful and interesting to anyone who knows less than you and wants to solve those same challenges.

Will you be a better expert next year? In five years? In ten years? Of course. But do you have to wait until then to start serving people in a bigger way? By waiting to share our knowledge until we are 'good enough' - whatever that means - we are actually doing a disservice to all the people we are not helping. Writing a book will give more people access to your skills and knowledge. Not writing a book keeps that knowledge to yourself and the limited number of people you currently work with.

Regardless of what other books are already written about your subject, no one has your exact experience or insight around the topic no matter how many years they have been doing it. We can say that pretty confidently because we're pretty certain that you're the only version of you out there and therefore your thoughts, your expertise, your knowledge, your experience is entirely unique. And your voice and your understanding of things will resonate and connect with a certain group of people. To be fair, it will also disconnect with a different group of people but, as we've said before, seeing as there are more than 7 billion people on this planet, even if your way of seeing things only connects with one in a million, that's more than 7000 people who will love what you say and they will want to be your client. For most practitioners and experts, 7000 people is more clients than they'll ever see in a lifetime so one in a million is not to be sniffed at!

With this in mind, and remembering that your book is merely a business tool rather than the pinnacle of your career, it might help explain why you should write your own book even if your teacher, guru,

The sad truth is that most people running a business have never been trained in business.

master, industry expert does not have one. The sad truth is that most people running a business have never been trained in business. Instead they have been trained in their expertise or skills and typically end up copying the business model used by everyone else in their profession, who also have never been trained in business. It is quite literally a case of the blind leading the blind with typically business practices and beliefs based on nothing other than, 'this is what everyone else is doing'.

When you view your business from this perspective, do you really want to hold yourself back by fitting in with everyone else? If other experts don't understand why they should write a book, is that any reason for you not to? Remember, you will help more people with your skills if the world knows you actually have skills. Staying the world's best kept secret will not help you make a difference. Having your own book and using it effectively to grow your business will enable you to reach far more people so you can have a bigger impact whilst also making a whole lot more money.

No one will buy my book or even want it for free...no one will read it...there are so many books in the world, why write another...
...insert limiting belief around your book here...

Let's get real with each other here; it is very unlikely that your book is going to become a New York Times Best-seller.

Sorry to burst that bubble but it's a seldom discussed truth that writing the next million-copy runaway best-seller is about as likely as winning the lottery. We're not saying it won't happen but the sad truth is that very few of the books written each year ever sell more than 500 copies. And only a very small percentage of authors make enough money to live on the proceeds of their writing.

Whilst depressing, this is exactly why writing your book is just the first step. Learning how to use it effectively to boost your business is what most authors fail to do. For example, Chris and Karene's best-selling book, *Grow Your Heart Centred Business: From Passion to Profit* has probably sold about 500 copies and made them a few thousands pounds at most from book sales. However, by successfully using their book in their business, they have created more than £300,000 to date in new client sales from this marketing tool in the last 2 years. Not a bad return on the 3 and a half weeks it took them to write and publish it!

Authors don't make money from books. However, properly trained business owners do. The key is to recognise the book is not about you! Which might sound strange since we've said your book needs to be based on your expertise and knowledge. This is still true but to be effective, your book can't just be a pamphlet or brochure about you and your business. It needs to address the problems and challenges that your clients face and provide them with solutions.

Only once they understand how you can help them, will people care about you and what you do. This might sound negative and selfish but actually it's just a basic human fact. Our brains are hardwired to look for what helps us almost to the exclusion of everything else.

'No one cares what you do, until they understand what you can do for them.'

So your book needs to solve people's problems. This is where your knowledge and expertise comes in and why people will want to buy or read your book. Once they understand that you can help them, then they will want to get to know you. This is where your personal story comes into play. Once people feel connected with you as a person, they will feel safe to take the next step of working with you, which is where the true money lies.

I don't have any idea what to write...
...insert limiting belief around ability here...

The biggest block for most 'wannabe' authors is the blank page. That looming feeling of pressure and blankness that stops most people getting started. And unfortunately, that first step in anything is both the hardest and the most important. Once you've started something, it is so much easier to continue so even if you're not sure what you're going to write overall, the secret is actually to just get started with something and it'll grow from there. Of course it is a lot more comforting and easier to have the exact plan for your book, along with chapter headings and mapped out content, worked out before you start, and this is something we help our clients create and detail in the following chapters. However, for most people, this is too big a step to achieve on their own.

So instead of focusing on writing a book and facing the dreaded blank page, what if you focused instead on what you do every day in your business? Consider what you say each day to your clients...chances are there's a lot of advice, instruction and general expertise being expressed in most of your conversations. And it probably comes out without you really even having to think about it because this is your area of expertise and you do it day in and day out. Whilst you might dismiss this as unimportant, it is actually exactly what could be used to create a very valuable and easy to read book. Sharing your day-to-day knowledge and advice would be engaging and powerful for people who are dealing with the same challenges as your clients and it would effortlessly position you as an expert in your field, which is a key aim for your book.

To give you some ideas, consider the following questions...

What are the 5 most common things you say to your clients?
What are the 5 most common questions clients ask you?
What are the 5 key questions your clients should be asking but rarely do?

What are the 5 most frequent challenges clients have before they work with you?

These are all topics you probably experience and speak about every day in your business. Writing some of these down and using these as your starting point will make it much easier to get going and will easily fill several pages at least. Once you have something, it is easier to continue and add more even if at this point you don't know what that 'more' is. The key is getting started in a way that is easy for you. The more your book informs and supports the challenges people are currently experiencing, the more impressed people will be with it.

Think of how you could serve your potential clients. In reality, your book could be that simple…'The 5 questions clients should ask before engaging a …(enter your profession)…' Providing advice to people on how to pick their expert would be massively valuable and help you stand out from all the other experts in your area because it shows you care more about your clients than you do about closing a sale!

If all this makes sense but you're still not sure what to write, forget about writing a big book and start with a small book. Any book is better than no book and even 20 pages of good content is enough to get you started. It's not about the number of pages each book has, it's about producing a tool you can use effectively to achieve your goals.

To give you some examples of e-books Chris and Karene wrote before their first #1 best-seller:

15 Completely Free Ways to Look Younger and Feel Better for Longer

7 Typical Business Mistakes made by Complementary Health Practitioners

The Networking Success Checklist: Are you making the most of your networking?

These e-books were all 20-40 pages long and were much quicker to produce than a full-sized book. However, despite being small and e-books rather than paperbacks, they were still useful tools for helping build Chris and Karene's award-winning training company, Heart Centred Business.

Ultimately, the goal of your book is to open up conversations with interested parties about topics related to your expertise. As long as you use it effectively, you can achieve the results you want with any size book, although, obviously, the bigger the book (within reason), the more impressive it is and the more valuable it will be to your business, provided of course it is filled with useful content that will help your readers overcome challenges. If you are still stuck for ideas, in the next chapter we specifically provide some tried-and-tested book topics and ideas that you could use successfully to get started.

Why would I give everything away for free...I have to hold back my secrets otherwise people will steal them...if I put my expertise in a book, people will stop paying for my services... ...insert limited belief around value, scarcity and money mindset here...

Resisting putting your 'good stuff' into a book is a big obstacle for most business owners. It gets even worse when we tell them they will mostly be giving their book away for free and so will earn little to no money from book sales!

However, as we've mentioned once or twice, most authors never make much money, regardless of what they try to sell their book for, so the ticket price of your book is irrelevant. Therefore, why not selectively give it away and get a lot more clients and a lot more money instead?

As we've mentioned once or twice, most authors never make much money.

At first glance it seems absurd that you should win new customers with free knowledge of all things. Why give away secrets for free? It's simple: exactly this marketing principle has been used for centuries in many industries and has been very successful.

Free knowledge will not cause people with a real problem to suddenly stop having difficulties because no matter how good the advice is, most people won't follow it or implement it. This is because there are two types of people in the world:

Do It Yourself (DIY) and Done For Me (DFM).

DIY'ers are the people who want to figure out how to do things themselves. They are the type of people who will read a book or spend hours on YouTube learning how to do or fix something.

DFM'ers are the opposite. They would rather pay someone else to do it for them. The less involvement they have the better.

Some examples...

In the fitness world:

DFM'ers would hire a Personal Trainer.

DIY'ers would watch YouTube videos and create their own programme

In the fine dining world:

DFM'ers go to the Michelin Star restaurant

DIY'ers watch Masterchef to learn how to create their own 5-star dining experience

In the home/building world:

DFM'ers hire a tradesperson to fix things up around the house

DIY'ers try and fix things themselves and read/watch/learn how they could do it better

In business/entrepreneurism:

DFM'ers hire a business coach or mentor to teach them what they don't know and to short cut their journey

DIY'ers try to figure things out on their own by testing out new things they've heard about

Everyone is on this DIY-DFM spectrum somewhere. Depending on the circumstances we are all DIY or DFM to some degree. Chris happily admits that Karene does all the DIY around their house. He is a very strong DFM and will happily leave DIY for Karene or a tradesperson to do.

Your book will appeal to both DIY'ers and DFM'ers, but with very different outcomes.

The DIY'ers will love it, read it from cover to cover and use what you suggest to help themselves. These people are not likely to become your clients because they don't want someone to do it for them, they want to do it themselves.

However, the DFM'ers will look at your book, perhaps read a few pages and love it but they'll rather contact you directly so you can solve their problems for them, rather than doing the work themselves. These people are the ones who are going to want to work with you and are likely to be your perfect clients. So ironically, the people who are unlikely to actually read your book are the ones who will be most inspired by it to become paying clients!

The people who are unlikely to actually read your book are the ones who will be most inspired by it to become paying clients!

This is why it's important to put your good stuff and special secrets in your book. Along with attracting the DFM people to work with you, it'll give support and guidance to the people who are never going to become your client - the DIY'ers. Though they won't want to work with you, they will become great marketers for you and happily recommend you to other people provided your book has been useful for them. Whilst this all makes logical sense, the fear that still stops some authors from sharing all their knowledge in their books is because they are afraid that other professionals might steal their knowledge and become their competition.

It is true that there are some unscrupulous people out there who will take your material and try and pass it off as their own. We have had a lot of coaches and business owners do this to us over the years. They attend our events and training, or read our books and then we see them on social media posting our concepts and strategies as their own and trying to build their own business training company. Whilst this is of course annoying, it is definitely not competition to us and is actually flattering if you think about it differently... they thought highly enough of what we teach to steal it and use it for themselves!

No one is ever going to be as successful as you are at using your skills, your strategies or your knowledge because they don't have your experience or understanding. Knowledge without the experience of how best to apply it doesn't work well and will not build any long-term success. Furthermore, they will not come across as such a credible expert because you have the book backing you up whilst they don't.

So when it happens and people steal or copy your 'secret sauce', see it as the poor imitation that it is, laugh instead of cry, and take it as a compliment that you are doing well enough that other people see that being like you is the easy route to success!

IN CLOSING...

Writing your own book will allow you to act from a position of strength in every contact with customers, partners and the general public. You'll benefit from various obvious and hidden advantages that far outweigh any concerns and objections around writing a book, such as:

- natural authority because if you have a book, you must be an expert!
- easier sales and comparatively higher turnover
- personal brand development and more effective long-term self-promotion
- easy access to new customers
- invitations as a speaker
- more chances of being mentioned exclusively in the press
- numerous interesting new contacts
- the ability to open different and higher level conversations with more people
- greater opportunity of partnerships and joint ventures
- better connections at higher levels of companies and organisations

Bottom line is, when it comes to writing a book, as we mentioned before, mindset is a huge influence, and as we heard from Henry Ford before, 'Whether you think you can, or whether you think you can't, you're absolutely right.'

CHAPTER 4

5 book ideas that everyone could implement immediately

You make anything by writing - C.S. Lewis

The last chapter has worked through all of the possible limiting beliefs you might have to writing a book and we get it that you may still be lacking inspiration. We talk to people every day who understand and agree how powerful a book is as a strategic business and marketing tool and yet still lack a concrete idea to get started with.

Typically we have lots of ideas and lots of confidence when it's just theory. Yet, when it becomes reality all ideas disappear or we don't think they're good enough. For many people, a book is a huge, insurmountable mountain of text. Faced with this mammoth task, how could you possibly come up with something that would fill the pages and generate the results that you're after?

Fear not, this chapter will provide you with a ready source of inspiration and more than that, some topics that you could use to get started. Something to remember here is that we aren't looking for a general book idea but rather a book that will showcase you and/or your business. This actually makes it much easier to narrow down the more successful ideas even if there are thousands or indeed hundreds of thousands of permutations you could create with your unique perspective.

How is that possible you may be thinking?

It is possible because we are all different and we have all had different experiences. Even if you have chosen a popular topic that has already been written about extensively, your perspective, your writing style and the things you emphasise will be different and interesting because no one else is you. For example, the theme of this book you're reading now is not unique: there are lots of books in the marketplace on how to write a book and become an author. However, what is unique about this book is that we aren't focused on the book, we are all about what you do with it once you have it aso you can create different and better results.

One of the reasons we have had success with our systems is because we make things straightforward. We acknowledge the obstacles and then find a way through, around, over or under them. Many of our clients, recognising the impact of books, are using their books as a platform to promote themselves or their business. They're having more conversations and ultimately getting more credibility and clients and it all started with them having an idea.

What topics could you tackle in your first book? Take a look at the following ideas to inspire your own creativity. Each of them can be adapted and implemented to your own needs immediately.

CONCEPT #1. YOUR CORE BUSINESS/SKILLS - BECAUSE YOU KNOW YOUR BUSINESS INSIDE OUT

Businesses solve problems and people within businesses also solve problems. It doesn't matter what industry you come from. It doesn't matter what you offer. It doesn't matter whether you run a service-based company, sell a product, or if you are an employee. You solve problems in exchange for payment or a salary. If you were to write a book that provided some of these solutions, your potential clients would understand how you could help them, recognise you as an expert and be curious to learn more.

> **Businesses solve problems and people within businesses also solve problems.**

The process to turning this into a book can be as simple as this:

1. Get clear on your viewpoint on your chosen subject (the area of your expertise).

2. Understand what solution your clients are actually looking to get.

3. Review the key challenges and problems your clients have.

4. Present HOW your clients can get past their problem to create the solution they want.

These simple steps will produce the key sections of your book and will appeal exactly to your ideal clients. Here's some examples to make it more real:

If your company offers food supplements...

1. You are probably convinced that food supplements help people become healthier, more energised and feel better.

2. Your clients want to feel younger and have more energy.

3. Your clients are fed up with feeling tired and lethargic, they don't know what to do and there's too much to choose from in the health stores.

4. The key supplements you recommend for health and energy, why you recommend them and where to get them.

If you are a real estate agent and help people find and finance their own homes...

1. You most likely believe that homes are a great investment.
2. Your clients want the security and pride that comes from owning their own home.
3. Your clients are frustrated with paying rent to someone else and feeling insecure.
4. Where and how to find a good estate agent and mortgage broker, what to ask them and what to expect on the journey.

If you run a digital marketing agency...

1. You probably think that clever online marketing is the very best way to make businesses more successful.
2. Your clients want to increase their number of sales and generate more revenue.
3. Your clients are frustrated that they don't have enough clients, don't earn enough money and feel like the world's best kept secret.
4. How to find a good digital marketing agency, what to ask them and what to expect in terms of cost vs return on investment.

Pretty straightforward right?

It's pretty much summarising what you do with your clients and what you get asked every single day. The key is to put yourself in the reader's position and focus on what they want to know.

If you are a business owner, the reader you are focused on is your ideal client. Picture them clearly in your mind as we discussed in Chapter 2 and focus your writing on how to help them solve their problems.

If you are an employee, the reader you are focused on is your existing boss and your potential future bosses. What do they need to know or understand about you and their business to see you as someone they can promote to get the job done?

We, as multi-bestselling authors, have all used this topic idea successfully in our books and many of our clients have chosen to use this format also to share their business systems or skills with the world. This book you're reading now is an example of this 'core business' topic brought to life, detailing why and how you too can write, and more importantly, use a book for success.

One of our clients, Janice, has a book specifically on recipes and tips to provide a drug-free solution for reducing migraines. This book has a very specific target audience and is a popular read for Janice's target market in her business. It gives them some ideas and knowledge for how to help themselves as well as next steps for how they might be able to work with Janice and get an even better result.

What might this be for you? What problem do you solve for your clients/stakeholders? Can you easily describe this and tell some stories along the way? If so, then perhaps this is the idea for you?

CONCEPT #2. LEARNING FROM MISTAKES – GET BACK WHAT YOU PAID FOR YOUR LEARNING

The second book idea, which everyone can implement immediately, is to share your biggest mistakes. We have all made mistakes in our careers, businesses, relationships, everyday choices. We all learn far more from our mistakes than we do our successes, so sharing your mistakes will allow people to accelerate their own journeys. As most people are looking for the 'shortcut' this is a very popular topic area.

> **We all learn far more from our mistakes than we do our successes.**

Also, any mistakes that you have made, are going to be very unique to your life experiences which makes them interesting reading. Most people would much rather sweep any negative experience under the carpet and deny any semblance of failure. However, we all know that mistakes are part of life and being human. Pretending to have never messed up is inauthentic and will put people off your story.

Being prepared to be vulnerable and share your mistakes in your book will connect you with your audience which will allow you to turn your mistakes into income. You will also allow your customers/stakeholders a unique insight into 'you', and given that people buy from/work with people that they know, like and trust, this will allow you to start building that all important relationship.

In truth, whilst our mistakes are interesting and potentially very entertaining, it is what we learn from them and how we overcome adversity that is the really interesting part. Again, what you learn will be unique to you and just sharing this may well inspire others in their lives and journeys. Much of the success of social media and reality TV is the obsession that we have as humans to watch others. Writing a book about your mistakes and subsequent learnings taps into this demand.

If, perhaps, you don't think that just your mistakes are enough for a book then you could combine your mistakes with other 'common' mistakes that you see your friends, colleagues or customers make. This will all make for compelling reading.

Chris and Karene's business, Heart Centred Business, was built on their mistakes and subsequent successes in business. Their book *Grow Your Heart Centred Business* outlines this with the specific intent of providing their customers with cautionary tales and short cuts so they can grow their businesses more quickly.

What mistakes have you made and learnt from? Could this be your starting point or perhaps a key couple of chapters to get you going?

CONCEPT #3. ANSWER YOUR CUSTOMERS' QUESTIONS

If you aren't inspired by what you offer, perhaps shift this perspective to the needs and desires of your customers? People ask questions to understand and to fulfil a need or desire. If you have been in business for a while then chances are you will have a long list of questions your customers frequently ask you. Similarly, if you manage staff you will also have a list of their most common questions people ask you. If you have a successful or unsuccessful relationship, you may even have a list of questions that friends have asked you over the years, or perhaps a particular hobby that everyone wants to know about like how to pick wine for a dinner party, spinning wool, golf or football.

The reality is we all have a huge base of questions we have come across in life that we have never considered as a source of inspiration or content for a book. Yet, if you have answered these questions for people, or participated in the ensuing conversations, then you have inadvertently created a 'how to' guide for other people in your industry, job or situation.

Without realising it, you have actually created the content for your first book.

Keeping it really simple, you can even format your book as an answer to those questions.

For example:

'The seven most frequent questions that customers ask.'

'The top 10 answers for your team to succeed.'

'The 5 things I wish I knew before I...'

Whatever number you choose will depend on how in-depth the answers to these questions are. You may even find you end up with much higher numbers, like us when we wrote the 'Top 50 Places to Network' and our '100 Ways to Get More Clients'.

There are no stupid questions, as they provide insight into how people think about topics and what they struggle with. If you need further evidence of this, the entire series '...for Dummies' highlights how popular this idea is and yet, there are still unanswered questions out there.

CONCEPT #4. AN EXPERT WITH A UNIQUE SYSTEM IS ALWAYS THE BEST ADVISOR

You are the expert, you know it. This is your opportunity to demonstrate your expertise by providing added value with your tips and secrets you may not otherwise reveal.

By sharing this insider knowledge, your credibility is established and your customers feel like they are sharing your secrets. You may think this is giving away all of the good stuff and it is. However, even with your secrets, chances are people won't use them or take the time to implement them and if they do, you will still get the credit.

Whatever makes you unique is great content for a book.

This is your opportunity to showcase yourself or your organisation, to talk about your company and point out that you offer a perfect solution for your customers' concerns.

You might describe what exactly your offer looks like and why you have designed it that way. You will certainly be able to explain convincingly why your offer is by far the best for your clients, providing helpful stories along the way to further demonstrate this. One of our clients at the time of writing this was doing just that with her book on gut health, told from her experiences with her clients and inspired by her father's battle with bowel cancer. She has already started standing out with her clients and her book isn't even finished.

As a 'expert' author, you can make a very detailed sales pitch to your clients throughout your book either directly or indirectly. There is no other marketing medium that gives you a comparable chance.

Whatever makes you unique is great content food a book. Maybe, you have developed a completely unique manufacturing process that results in unique product features or unrivalled quality. Or you may have a consulting methodology that helps customers find exactly the right product or service? Your special solution has not only proven itself thousands of times in practice, but also none of your competitors can offer it? Maybe you have just given a sales procedure that is common in your industry a particularly memorable name? Any or all of these make for an interesting read and position you well with your existing or future clients.

Possible titles are, for example:

'The proven three-step system to find the most suitable food supplement'

'The revolution of PPC marketing - the John Doe method'

'The real estate valuation system V-I-L-L-A'

'The M-M neuro marketing positioning model by John Doe'

With such a book title, you will not only immediately stand out from the masses of standard 'expert books', but it will also help you with all your other communication and sales measures.

CONCEPT #5. SUPPORT YOUR CLIENT'S DECISION MAKING

Another book idea is to support people with their decision making. Many people find it difficult to make decisions and the popularity of magazines such as 'Choice' and 'Which?' highlight the demand for such advice. This is where you can highlight the expertise you have built up over the years providing insight into what is actually important. There are often a lot of aspects to consider when making a wise choice. When purchasing a used car, for example, there are countless details to consider, otherwise you might end up with a nasty surprise.

Customers are all the more grateful if you, as an expert, help them with such decisions and save them from expensive mispurchases. Some example titles using this idea could be:

'Seven factors to consider when buying a house'

'How to find the right online marketing agency'

'How to find the right food supplement for you'

'10 Factors to consider when choosing a Mentor'

Even with this ready advice in your book, your ideal customers may seek you out for specific guidance because they are looking for a shortcut or additional reassurance or a premium service particularly if they are more of a DFM (Done For Me) than DIY (Do It Yourself).

Part of any decision-making process is usually a consideration of price. What is the pricing structure in your industry? How are services and prices put together? What costs should the customer expect if he is interested in a certain solution? How can a customer compare the prices and services of different providers? Are there hidden costs that are swept under the carpet in calculations and instead show up later as 'extras'? Customers want to know all this.

For an estate agent in South West London, you could write a book about local estate prices: 'House prices for single-family homes 2022 in South West London' would be a possible title. In this book, readers would then learn how real estate prices have developed in South West London specifically, how they are made up, what negotiating scope clients have in this region of London, etc.

For an online marketing agency, a suitable title would be 'What does it cost to hire an online marketing agency?' or 'Online marketing agencies in the UK: prices 2022'. This compendium would inform its readers about the price structure they should expect when hiring an online marketing agency in the UK, what services are common there, how the agency selection and contract awarding process usually works, etc.

As you can see, you can easily adapt this book idea to local or even regional markets and thus very precisely to your ideal customers.

You can also explain to your clients which service components are included in your prices and what is behind the services in detail resulting in far more educated clients and increased credibility and trust in you as a business partner.

Now that you have some ideas, how do we turn these into a book? If you have been taking notes or been particularly inspired in this chapter, fantastic; the next chapter is all about developing these ideas into a structure and ultimately your book.

CHAPTER 5

Success system:
The fastest way from the idea to the finished book

The first draft of everything is shit
- Ernest Hemingway

We have found, as have many others, that success is about doing the right things in the right order, which is all about systems. Love them or hate them, systems or repeatable ways of doing things that avoid mistakes, or short-cut them, are key if you want to succeed more quickly in anything. We have learned from our mistakes and successes and those of our clients and eventually developed a system for book projects. Over the years, we have continued to improve our system and even founded a business, HCB Publishing, that helps successful entrepreneurs, experts, trainers, students and school graduates to write, publish and more importantly, market a book in the shortest possible time with the help of our system.

For us, our system enables anyone to write their own personal success book: 'Your Book as a Business Booster'.

We're giving our 3-step system away in this book. As we explained, we know that some of our readers will want to do this themselves and we also know that even with the knowledge some won't. We would recommend you do this with your book too. Give away the good stuff and reach more people and those that want or need your support even with all the answers in your book will still want the shortcut or a personalised service. Having read your book, these clients will be better educated and in our experience are much more fun to work with because they get better results and your work with them is all about implementation rather than just teaching. And even if they haven't read your book, they are more prepared to work for the outcome with your support. When your clients get better and faster results, your reputation will spread. This is a great virtuous circle that you create when you give first.

> **We're giving our 3-step system away in this book.**

Just as we know that not everyone will take action as a result of reading this book, we also know that you will be tempted to do things differently and to try it 'your way'. Many of our clients have done this and guess what, it works best when you just follow the system of what is tried-and-tested to work rather than trying to reinvent the wheel. We also know you probably are having a 'Yes, but...' moment so by all means go ahead and try if you must, however, know that you will get the best results when you follow the system.

So what exactly do you share when you share a 'system'? We aren't expecting you to explain all of your techniques, timescales etc in minute detail. Rather, think of what you are providing in your book as the governing philosophy that will dictate how to apply the skills and knowledge necessary to achieve your typical outcomes. Clarity, simplicity and being succinct are all vitally important for a well-understood and appealing system.

A system needs to explain the principles of what you do and how you will give your clients/readers the results they want.

With the unique system 'Your Book as a Business Booster' you can write and publish and most importantly, make money from your professional book in only 90 days, even if you don't think you are a gifted writer, copywriter or 'word person'.

Our system consists of 3 steps:

Prepare

Persist

Profit

Our system consists of 3 steps:

1. Prepare

2. Persist

3. Profit

1. PREPARE

This step is all about setting yourself up for success. We mentioned our 2-step approach of plan/do. This is most definitely the planning phase of the approach which will enable you to reduce your writing time and also ensure that you are starting with the end in mind so that you can ultimately profit from your book whether that be in your career or business.

2. PERSIST

This step is most definitely the 'doing'. This is about writing or recording your content in line with the structure you will have developed during the 'Prepare' step. It will also ensure that you complete all the steps that people either forget or just don't realise exist in going from idea through to published book. This 'Persist' step might not sound like a fun step and for some of you it won't be, however, writing a book, whilst straightforward, will require some effort and we like to be up front about these things rather than hiding them in the fine print. Something to consider if this step feels too much like hard work is that you make it someone else's problem and hire support to get your book written for you, however, more about this later.

3. PROFIT

In this step, you have a published book which is fabulous, however this alone will not make you a success. We talked before about the fact that it isn't about the book. There are a series of next steps that you will need to undertake to make the most of your book. This step is where you market your book and use it effectively to achieve the outcome that you set out in your 'Prepare' step whether this is a promotion or new job, new clients or all of the above. It is this step that turns you from an author to successful author whio makes money.

In the remainder of this chapter we will cover Step 1 and some of Step 2. The remaining chapters of this book will then cover off the rest of Step 2 and Step 3.

PREPARE

You can't just write any old book because that won't help you create the results you want. You will only be able to unleash the full power of this great business and marketing tool if you write a book that is fully aligned with your business goals, your brand and your vision. Only a really cleverly designed book that is used effectively will give you and/or your company the advantages mentioned above. To help you achieve this, we need to start with the end in mind. What is it that you want to achieve with your book? How will it support you, your career or business?

There are 2 components to this step:

1. Your vision of success.
2. Your book architecture or structure.

YOUR VISION OF SUCCESS

Looking first at component one, your vision of success, we need to get clear as to what success is for you. No doubt having read this far, you will have an idea and you could jump straight into creating content. However, if you do this, it will take you longer and probably result in wasted time. Rather your first step is to get clear on your vision of success. Success for you as an author and success for your readers. We are very clear as to what success looks like for us and our business. You will have also noticed that at the beginning of this book we identified three possible outcomes for you, the reader, and we would expect you to do similar.

Develop a business plan for your book.

Develop a business plan for your book. It is, after all, a product or service and all good products and services are clear on what problem they are solving and who they are solving it for and what outcome they are likely to get. What is the potential size of the market, who are your competitors, what opportunities are there to add value and stand out and what weaknesses do you need to address? Remember Person, Problem, Solution in Chapter 2? If you have forgotten perhaps go back and remind yourself as this will provide you with the fundamentals.

Here are some key questions you should ask yourself to help you focus on the concept of your book:

- Why do you want to write a book?
- What exactly do you want to achieve with your book?
- What would be the ideal outcome for you?
- What do you want your readers to believe after reading your book?
- What will make your book special?
- How does your book differ from comparable books in terms of content, language, structure, graphic or design?
- How do you want others to talk about your book?
- How would one of your readers recommend your book in brief?

As you can see, this step is about the big picture, the philosophy behind the content, the core themes and statements of your book, and also your central argument. This will allow you to better define what needs to be included or perhaps kept for the next book. It will stop you from going off on too many tangents and it allows you to get your marketing messages clear from the beginning which means if you have other people supporting you with writing or creating your book, they will also be on the same page as you (no pun intended).

Once you are clear on your vision, you can write the text or a 'blurb' for your book. With your clear vision and answers to the questions above, you will be able to capture that catchy text on the back of the book that speaks to your readers and tells them what to expect. Remember people pay attention when they know what is in it for them.

Even though you will probably not adhere to this first draft in the end, it will help you to gain a content focus for your book and to determine its structure. You can also share this blurb with your potential market for feedback. Perhaps you share it in conversation with your customers or email to your list or on your social media, the medium is irrelevant as long as you share it. The great thing about sharing this intent is it starts your marketing process, people are now aware you are writing a book and might even want to pre-order. You will start getting an idea of who might be curious about your book. You may even be able to generate curiosity and sell some of your services just from these book 'ideas'.

By planning your book in this way, you create a really valuable strategic business and marketing tool before you even have a book.

For some people this might actually be enough, they make some sales from this idea and that gets them momentum in their business and they are off. Obviously, we would prefer that you keep going and see this for what it is, a first step and an opportunity to be paid and support more people. This is a big win as being paid as an author before you write anything is usually only possible if you get a publishing deal, whereas with our clients it is standard procedure.

So if you do make money from just this initial stage, celebrate and then keep going because you'll be able to create a whole lot more in the long run by following the whole system.

If you don't manage to make money from this initial stage that's ok because you are still building curiosity and your database of potentially interested parties who will help you make money long term.

So, what comes next?

YOUR BOOK ARCHITECTURE OR STRUCTURE

Next you should turn more seriously to the content i.e., the structure of the content and the central line of argument for your book. The right book architecture is crucial to being able to take people on a journey through your book so they engage, learn and enjoy the experience.

Now you might be thinking that this all sounds daunting, however, you have already created your vision board. Starting with this vision, answer these questions:

- What do you need to write in order to realise your goals with your book?
- What are the central statements of your book?

Based on the answers to these core questions, you will work out the structure of your book - the chapters and subchapters, i.e., the most important statements or thesis of your book as well as their justifications.

For example, in writing this book, we knew we wanted people to realise that writing a book was possible, that they could use their book to create massive financial success, and that there is a system and shortcuts along the way for all of this to happen. So, we got a blank page and wrote down all of the things that people would need to know for us to have achieved this goal. This list included:

Why write a book?

Why most people don't make any money from being an author?

What does a book give you?

What is marketing?

What are all the reasons people don't write books?

Why do most authors fail in business?

What is the system for writing?

What do you do once you have a book?

And under all of these headings we wrote the stories and ideas that support these main topics.

With your book, you could start in the same way. Put your goal in the middle or at the top of the page depending on whether you like going down a page or using a mindmap. Write down all the main arguments to support your goal and also all of the objections and reasons that stop people or the excuses they have.

This will then provide you with your main chapters. You then put your statements in a logical order and create your chapter headings. If you manage to make them more concise and formulate them in such a way that your readers become curious, all the better!

First, work on being happy with your chapter headings for the main chapters. Next, go one level deeper and create sub-headings for your chapters. These sub-headings mark out the 'subchapters' within each chapter. These subchapters are the key components or messages within each chapter and will further support your vision of what that chapter is aiming to achieve. You're aiming for around 6 subchapters per chapter.

For example, your subchapters could include your own stories, recognised knowledge that you describe in your own words, or where you contribute your experiences or views regarding the main statement of the chapter.

For the last step, you collect key words for each main chapter and subchapter that should appear in the body text. These keywords will prompt you to remember what you want to include when it comes to actually writing the content.

All of the other content such as Table of Contents, Acknowledgements, Foreword, Glossary or Bibliography are inserted at the very end.

If this is too confusing described in words, let's go with some pictures to help clarify what we're saying. The basic structure of your book could look something like this:

CHAPTER 1	CORE MESSAGE 1
SUBCHAPTER 1.1	SUBCHAPTER STATEMENT 1 ON CORE MESSAGE 1
SUBCHAPTER 1.2	SUBCHAPTER STATEMENT 2 ON CORE MESSAGE 1

SUBCHAPTER 1.3	SUBCHAPTER STATEMENT 3 ON CORE MESSAGE 1
SUBCHAPTER 1.4	SUBCHAPTER STATEMENT 4 ON CORE MESSAGE 1
SUBCHAPTER 1.5	SUBCHAPTER STATEMENT 5 ON CORE MESSAGE 1
SUBCHAPTER 1.6	SUBCHAPTER STATEMENT 6 ON CORE MESSAGE 1

KEYWORDS FOR CHAPTER 1...

Keyword

Keyword

Keyword

CHAPTER 2	**CORE MESSAGE 2**
SUBCHAPTER 2.1	SUBCHAPTER STATEMENT 1 ON CORE MESSAGE 2
SUBCHAPTER 2.2	SUBCHAPTER STATEMENT 2 ON CORE MESSAGE 2
SUBCHAPTER 2.3	SUBCHAPTER STATEMENT 3 ON CORE MESSAGE 2

SUBCHAPTER 2.4	SUBCHAPTER STATEMENT 4 ON CORE MESSAGE 2
SUBCHAPTER 2.5	SUBCHAPTER STATEMENT 5 ON CORE MESSAGE 2
SUBCHAPTER 2.6	SUBCHAPTER STATEMENT 6 ON CORE MESSAGE 2

KEYWORDS FOR CHAPTER 2...

Keyword

Keyword

Keyword

And so on...

From this rough content structure, a more detailed structure will then emerge in the further elaboration, which will look like this:

CHAPTER 1   CHAPTER STATEMENT 1

(as an inquisitive heading to generate curiosity)

Chapter introduction

(= shorthand collection of content of your own story, experience or other content that elaborates and supports the chapter statement and arouses curiosity for the following subchapters and chapters)

SUBCHAPTER 1.1   SUBCHAPTER STATEMENT 1

(as a catchy, perhaps even provocative heading)

Subchapter text 1.1

(= shorthand collection of content of your own story, experience or other content that further elaborates the chapter statement 1 or supports a partial aspect of chapter statement 1 presented in subchapter 1.1)

And so on...

With this structure in mind we then need to understand how many chapters and how much content you need to produce.

Ideally, your book needs to be a minimum of 100 pages so that the spine is big enough to hold the necessary detail such as the title and your name. This is what separates a 'real' book from something that is perceived as a pamphlet or brochure. 100 pages in a book approximately 50-60 A4 pages of text depending on font size. When we write our books we typically use a google doc as there are sometimes a number of us contributing to the same book so we can all do this simultaneously anywhere there is an internet connection. We

> Your book needs to be a minimum of 100 pages so that the spine is big enough to hold the necessary detail such as the title and your name.

typically use 11pt font and have each chapter starting on a new page for ease of use.

We also like writing action-oriented books, as, for us, the point of our books is to get people into action. We typically have a motivating quote at the beginning and a list of action steps at the end of each chapter just as we have in this book. Some of our clients do the same, others don't if it doesn't suit their content. A good place to start thinking about how you might structure chapters for your book is in other books...

- What books have you particularly enjoyed and why?
- What did they have in them?
- How were they structured?

Now you have your 'Goal' and your structure, you are ready to get on with writing. This will now be much easier as the structure will provide you the prompts and guidance so you can focus on producing content.

PERSIST

This step is all about writing and publishing and how you can do this most effectively in the shortest period of time. In the remainder of this chapter we will look at content creation and then the subsequent chapter will look specifically at publishing. As the name suggests however, this step will require work.

Sadly, we don't have a magic wand, however, we do have some shortcuts to share with you. That said, there is great satisfaction that comes from putting the work in and creating something yourself. Let's face it, if it was easy to write, publish and gain success from a book, everyone would be doing it. And even if we think everyone should be doing it and we have a system that can help them, we know most people won't. So given everyone isn't committed to writing a book, the fact that you are will be one of your key advantages.

THE WRITING PROCESS

With the structure in place it is now time to fill in the blanks. Normally, authors write their books one word at a time. This is a quiet, introspective process. If that suits you, great, you will just need to get on with it. Follow the guidelines already given and complete the individual chapters and subchapters of your book on the basis of the keywords and summary you have created.

If, however, you aren't a natural writer, then simply sitting down and trying to write will be an exhausting and often frustrating process. Chances are, you would fail right here and give up. However, you are holding a gold-plated system of support so you can write a book

If it was easy to write, publish and gain success from a book, everyone would be doing it.

and create all of the success that comes from it! Read on, as there are ways of making 'writing' much easier and in some instances you won't have to write anything at all.

There are four different approaches to content creation we've found that will get you a completed manuscript more quickly and easily:

1. Little and Often
2. Talk it through
3. Chat it through
4. Enlist support

Before we go into these approaches, all of them, perhaps with the exception of having a team do it all for you which is option 4, will still need you to find time and we're sure that you, like us, are already super busy. So before we explain the different approaches, let's find you some extra time so you have the greatest chance of success.

HOW CAN YOU HAVE MORE TIME?

Wanting more time is a universal desire of everyone we know. How many times have you said to yourself or a loved one, 'I'm sorry, I don't have time'? Fundamentally, the key reason we don't have time is because we fail to prioritise.

When we look at the challenge of not having enough time, this is primarily created by the fear we all have of 'missing out'. This Fear Of Missing Out has become so ubiquitous that we even have an acronym for it: FOMO. People become unconsciously terrified if they say 'No' to something or someone, they might miss out. This could be a missed client, a missed opportunity, a missed connection, a missed party, episode, drink or anything at all. It all comes down to a fear that if you miss out on something, you might miss out on being part of the tribe. Remember the fundamental fear in all of us, coming from caveman times, is the fear of rejection? If you're not part of the tribe, we feel at risk of dying, so we tend to say, 'Yes' to everything to avoid missing out. Knowing when to say 'No' is a critical step to free up time or make time.

Get clear on what you're doing things for by connecting to your 'Why'.

How do you know what to say 'No' to?

It's all about priorities. And how do we set priorities? Get clear on what you're doing things for by connecting to your 'Why' When you are clear on 'Why' you are doing something, you can more easily know what will move you forward towards your goals vs what is a distraction or something that supports other people's goals rather than your own. With this clarity, you will be able to make conscious decisions about how you are to spend your time, meaning you will prioritise certain actions over others.

As a set of action steps:

- Get clear on your 'Why' and your goals.
- Say 'Yes' to things that move you towards your goals.
- Say 'No' to things that don't.

We're not going to say it's always easy to stick to schedules, as it seems to be the human condition (or perhaps just ours) to try and do too much in too short a space of time. For example, writing this book has been a major priority for us. However, we don't have the luxury of locking ourselves away to write it. We have a child and extended family to support, multiple businesses to run, employees to manage and hundreds of clients to serve. To make this book happen, we had to make time. For us, this resulted in 3 weeks of some very late nights/early mornings, fitting in our writing around all of our other commitments in order to get it done.

Looking back, what made this book happen was single-minded focus and connecting with what this book will mean for our business, our clients, and, most importantly, what it might mean for you, the reader. This is how we managed to fit in what was needed to meet the unreasonable and unrealistic deadlines we set ourselves.

Speaking of deadlines, setting unreasonable and unrealistic deadlines can be a great way of creating time and fitting in impossible tasks. When we say unreasonable and unrealistic this refers to what most people would say when you tell them your goal. In life or business, if you only do what is reasonable or realistic, you are guaranteed a result of mediocrity at best. For example, 1 in 5 businesses fail in the first year and 50% of those businesses that survive year 1, fail before their 5th year. If you were starting a business today, this is a realistic and a reasonable assumption. Yet, our clients regularly create unreasonable results, precisely because they set 'unrealistic goals'.

Ruth, a Pilates Teacher, is a great example of this. In the first 4 months of going full time in teaching Pilates, she earned more than £7000 in a single month twice. Ruth's business success is unrealistic if you don't have proven systems to follow and a drive or 'Why' you want to make it happen.

Our actual goal for writing this book was to complete it in one week. This was the big unreasonable and unrealistic goal that we set to drive us to put the necessary effort in. However, we failed. We didn't manage to push ourselves or our schedule enough to make this happen. In the end it took us two weeks to write and one week more to self-edit before the manuscript was ready to send to our publisher. We failed to hit our target, yet setting such an unreasonable goal enabled us to achieve so much more than many people thought possible. The late nights, the extra stresses and challenges were all totally do-able because writing this book was an exciting process completely connected with our mission of creating 1000 Heart Centred millionaires. What goal would motivate you enough to be unreasonable and expect more from yourself?

Having done the exercise of setting goals for your book, it is possible you might need to do this for your business or perhaps even your life so you can be clear on your priorities. This will allow you to be clear on what to say 'Yes' to and even more importantly, what you need to say 'No' to.

NOW I HAVE TIME, HOW DO I FOCUS?

We have lots of ways to keep focused. Answering questions about why you are publishing a book in the first place is certainly a big help and yet, we are all human so life will happen and things will get in the way. Yes, there are the more extreme approaches of going somewhere remote to just write. However, you can still get distracted and it isn't always about sitting down and having a large continuous writing session. Little and often will often get things done more easily and often more quickly

CHUNK IT DOWN

Little and often will get things done more easily and often more quickly.

This is a very straightforward approach most people forget when faced with a big project. You can't climb a mountain all at once and you certainly can't eat a meal all at once. We take steps or mouthfuls, ideally one at a time. So, using this principle, work out your final word count or page count and an end date when you want your manuscript completed by. Once you know this, you can work out how many words or pages you need to write each day. This will give you small achievable goals. This is a great technique for anything really, the smaller and more manageable the steps or mouthfuls, the more likely you are to succeed and actually complete the actions that move you forward. Embrace dividing your book project into manageable chunks and get going.

SINGLE SONG ON REPEAT

At some point in high school, Karene's mother sent her on a study skills course. In addition to teaching mind mapping and other summary techniques, it was also mooted that baroque music or listening to anything by Bach is conducive to learning. Since this is corroborated by the wonderful movie 'The Incredibles' it absolutely must be true.

You may or may not like Bach, however having his music playing in the background is a great way to focus your mind. If your music tastes are different to this you can borrow our other effective method which is to play a single song on repeat. To write our book *Grow Your Heart Centred Business*, a 350-page beast, we listened to 'Non Stop' from the Hamilton soundtrack and also 'Walk Me Home' by P!nk.

For this book you're reading now, our chosen track to play on continuous repeat whilst writing is, 'All I know so far' by P!nk. What you choose is up to you, however, the repetition of the single song will get you into a focused mental state without distracting you and will assist you to concentrate for far longer than you would have expected.

Of course, you may still find you 'need' to dust under the sofa, eat, make endless cups of tea or endless other distraction techniques to justify not writing. Remember, it is all a choice. Connect to what you are writing for and make better choices on how you use your time. Once you are connected to something bigger than yourself, or can picture that final result of holding a complete book in your hand, or, better yet, handing it over to an excited customer, you will be back into content creation.

We say content creation vs writing as it isn't all about writing, so let's get back into the 4 key options, all of which you can mix and match as needed to assist you in completing your manuscript.

LITTLE AND OFTEN

This option is still you doing the writing, however, it is about doing it in a specific way to make it more easy and effective. If writing isn't for you then skip to the next options as they may be more suitable.

We talked about Chunking it Down above so hopefully you have put this in action and know what your daily writing task needs to be. Once you know this, set aside a time each day or each week depending on how quickly you want results and get writing. An added motivation for this is the concept of 'don't break the chain'. Doing it every day ensures there is growing pressure not to break the multi-day writing streak. Once the streak or chain is broken, even once, it is far easier to make excuses and 'break' it again in the future.

This technique is used very effectively in Alcoholics Anonymous and lots of habit forming approaches to ensure people keep going consistently. There are many ways to track your progress; for example, you may have a diary or calendar where you put ticks on it every time you successfully complete your required writing and you try and keep those ticks continuous. Just a little every day and you will soon have completed your manuscript without all of the frustration and anxiety.

TALK IT THROUGH OR CHAT IT THROUGH

If writing isn't for you, perhaps talking is? In both approach two and three, you simply speak your book! In other words, you tell a fictitious listener, or even better, a real listener, all the content you need for your book by saying exactly what comes into your head, based on your structure and your noted keywords.

If just talking feels too lonely then you may opt for getting your book sorted by interview. We will provide more detail in Option 4 how this can all be done for you as we do with some of our clients; however, assuming you are still going it alone then you will need to find a suitable person to interview you. The idea being that your 'interviewer' will ask you specific questions that will effectively help you to record the contents of your book step by step and in a structured way. This makes the process of writing your book enjoyable, playful and relaxed at the same time - almost like a familiar conversation with a customer. And remember, you could be your own interviewer for this process as well. You just need to do some extra preparation which would be key for ensuring that you stay on track if you are just recording the content by talking.

This makes the process of writing your book enjoyable, playful and relaxed.

Your interviewer should guide you through the previously planned book structure and ask you specific questions about the content of the individual chapters and subchapters and keep you talking.

Questions? Yes exactly, questions! They might be questions that encourage you to give examples or stories. This makes your presentation livelier and more credible. They can be questions about your experiences or judgements about certain issues. Your interviewer may also ask you for definitions or clarifications of terms that will make you describe in a more precise manner or provide a conclusion. Or they may ask you about disadvantages, particularly important aspects or frequent mistakes.

Ideally, your interview partner should be someone who is interested in your topic, who is intelligent, who thinks along with you, who has empathy and an overview, but who can also take the point of view of a very clueless reader.

This can be quite a demanding process, however, if done correctly will make creating your manuscript a fun and straightforward process. Here are some sample questions and suggestions from the multi-page interview checklist we developed for our clients to support this process:

- Tell me about the moment when you....!
- How did you feel when you...?
- What made you get into...?
- What are the particular advantages of...?
- What are the particular disadvantages of...?
- What should you keep in mind when...?
- What mistakes do people often make in this area?
- What do you wish more people knew about...?
- What should people look out for when selecting...?
- What's the most important thing to keep in mind when looking to solve...?

- Tell me about your most interesting client!
- What is the most common question people ask?
- What is the question people should be asking instead?

As with all things that seem straightforward, there are usually some simple things that people forget, so make sure you stick to your table of contents! Your interview partner must do the same. We guarantee that your interviewer will need to keep reminding you to stay focused on your topics and in the right order or the editing job will be significant.

Your interviewer will also be key in ensuring that you slow down if you get too excited or bring you back on topic if you digress. They will also be able to provide additional questions to perhaps trigger you if you don't deliver enough. That's important because it is far better to have too much than too little.

Your interviewer should keep asking you questions about a chapter or subchapter until your explanations are really completely understandable and coherent. If you can't do this in one go, just take breaks. That's what the pause button on recordings is for. We want to make sure that you have comprehensively covered everything and not forgotten anything.

Using these approaches for content creation, your words replace the keyboard or pen. If you don't mention something because it's natural for you in your professional environment, it doesn't have to be so for your readers - not even if they are fellow professionals - so make sure that you are explaining things in a way that anyone can understand. We like to think of this as ensuring a 10-year-old child could understand what you are explaining. If they can't, chances are you are being unnecessarily sophisticated and you may lose your readers' attention.

Also remember, what you don't say won't be recorded. This important content will be missing later in your book if you don't discover it during the revision. It is far better to over-deliver and talk about everything you could possibly want to include in your book as you can always edit it out later. Put yourself in the mind of your readers or your customers. They don't know what you know, so what do you need to include so that they can know and understand? Thoroughness and completeness are required here, as well as an interview partner who is on the ball.

By the way: linguistic fine-tuning is not important at this point. The only thing that counts is the content itself. And how much content do we need? We talked about needing enough content to fill a minimum of 100 pages, however, if you aren't typing your book, how much is enough?

People speak around 100 words per minute on average. A 200-page book contains about 30,000 words. Your audio recording should therefore be about 5 hours long. This might seem like a lot, however we tend to be more verbose when speaking so it might be that you need to record more than this 5 hours to then edit it back to the slick and succinct final product.

TURNING YOUR RECORDING INTO A TRANSCRIPT

After you have completed all the content for your book by talking or chatting it through in an interview, you should save the audio file and transcribe it. Transcription means nothing more than converting the audio data into text. Unfortunately, this also involves work that you either have to do yourself or outsource to a transcription service.

There are a number of different options for transcription, from using actual people through to programmes or apps. There are some programmes that type directly from your dictation and others that transcribe after the fact. If you Google 'transcription services' you'll see a wealth of options available. This is definitely a skilled task and not something we would suggest you do yourself, no matter how much of a DIYer you are as it can be very time consuming. Professional word processors and transcribers can be very quick in turning the spoken word into text and AI solutions can now be provide entire transcribed manuscripts in a matter of minutes.

If you are insistent on doing it yourself, how long this will take will depend on the length of the audio and your typing speed. Punctuation, spelling etc is not your primary focus rather just getting it typed is. Everything else can be fixed during editing.

If you have ever read a transcript you will know that it is unlikely to read like a high-quality book. However, it will be much easier for you to continue editing this rough manuscript than to start from scratch. Starting from something is always easier than starting from a blank page.

In our experience, it takes about 40 hours to revise a transcript or raw text into a first real draft of a manuscript. So with 5-10 hours recording audio this is 45-50 hours to get a first draft of a manuscript. By comparison, if you write your book the 'old-fashioned way' and actually write, it usually takes 300 to 500 hours. For many authors, it takes much longer.

Personally, we've done both routes and will continue to mix and match depending on the project. This is because, even with the speed advantages of audio recordings, sometimes, the slower act of writing is actually part of the thought process that solidifies the ideas into a readable book

How long it will take you to turn an audio transcription into a book depends on how extensive and structured your transcript is, what you expect of yourself and your content, what skills you have and how much routine you already have for such a task.

As for how you edit your transcription, we suggest that you read through the first sentences of your transcript. Decide for each sentence whether it contains information that is really important for your book. Is something important still missing? Then add it now.

Then successively revise the remaining sentences stylistically and for the first time with regard to spelling and punctuation.

During the proofreading and editing process shortly before layout, design and printing, the final correction is made. However, it is better if your manuscript is already comprehensible to everyone by this point. Then you can give it to a professional editor without getting too many questions or required revisions.

In this way, you revise all sentences, paragraphs and sections of your transcript until you have a very solid first draft of your book.

Bravo, the manuscript of your book is ready! Now you need to revise and correct it one final time. How does that work? We recommend a strategy that many professional authors use.

It's very simple: read your book aloud to yourself - slowly, sentence by sentence.

In this double role - reading aloud and listening - you will inevitably come across sentences that are difficult to understand, that sound strange, that are hard to read aloud or that don't really make sense. These are the sentences you should change. Finally, read them out loud again in connection with the previous and following sentence. Does it fit now? Great!

When you have finalised that, you have the finished book text in front of you. You've done it! Well, almost.

After a while, no matter how good you are at reading and listening to yourself, you become blind to what you are reading and you may assume that things are there when they are not. That's why we would also advise you to have your book professionally proofread before printing. After all, you don't write a book every day, but if you want to ensure high quality it is worth hiring a professional. There are plenty of options out there to find people and you may even enlist the support of family and friends who can also give you some advanced feedback. Karene's mother has read all of our

Have your book professionally proofread before printing.

books prior to printing and she is great at editing, however, we still get a professional proofreader to work their magic.

Like finding any tradesperson, there are always good and bad options and cheap and expensive. Work out what you actually need as with outsourcing anything, the more specific you can be, the better the result.

YOUR FINAL BOOK PRODUCTION APPROACH: ENLIST SUPPORT

Approach 4 is where all of these activities are done for you. If you are like us, the fact that this approach exists may give you hope that you can actually complete a book. Let's face it, all of the other approaches sound like and are hard work. It is possible though to find someone to support you through all of the activities.

Knowing how challenging content creation can be, and having struggled through this process ourselves, we have put together a team who are familiar with our system and understand what is necessary to get it done. Working with clients we provide all of these services in an end-to-end solution which dramatically cuts down your time commitment as well as the overall time to produce a manuscript. From ghost writer to editor, proofreader to book architect, there are many professional services available to get your book done for you, and most of them will be tax deductible business expenses.

Obviously, if you have already started the process of writing yourself and become stuck we can also support you, so get in touch so we can understand how to best do this.

Regardless of which option you choose, this step of the system is usually the most time consuming and also the most rewarding as at the end of this process you will have a completed manuscript ready for publishing. Publishing is still in the 'persist' step of the system and we will explain this in the next chapter. If you are taking action as you read this book then now is the time to put these suggestions into action and focus on your content. You can then come back to the subsequent chapters once you have your manuscript.

Congratulations! By now, you know what to do, have decided on which route you are going to take and hopefully are already in action making your book a reality. Keep in mind that despite all this effort to get a completed manuscript, it isn't about the book in the end. You are creating a super high-quality tool for building credibility and making money. Whatever route you take to get there, keep going until it's done. Like anything that requires effort and time, we, as humans often quit too soon, particularly, and ironically, if the end is in sight, so keep going, get it done and stand out as the expert we know that you are.

CHAPTER 6

Why you don't need a publisher to get your book published

Somewhere inside all of us is the power
to change the world - Roald Dahl

You may be reading this section prior to having a manuscript, or you may still be at the idea phase thinking you need to get someone to publish you and then they will pay you a big advance and life will be sorted. Yes, this is possible and so is buying a lottery ticket and winning multiple millions. Whilst we are all for optimism and good luck, we've found it far better to Create the results you want rather than wait for them to appear magically in your life.

Whilst it is definitely possible to find a publisher and have them market and sell your book for you, this is a lot harder to do than most people think. Many authors never find a publisher or agent willing to take on their book which

> Create the results you want rather than wait for them to appear magically in your life.

has lead to the massive rise in self-publishing. Seeing as it isn't about the book rather what you do with it that counts, we suggest going the self-publishing route. However, we want you to understand all your options before you take any action so in this chapter we'll explore what a publisher or publishing house actually does, why there are traditional publishers and what other options you have.

TRADITIONAL PUBLISHING

A publisher or publishing house is a kind of 'venture capitalist' which really just means they are an investor in book ideas. They consist of a group of specialists who help you turn your book idea into a finished book. The publishing staff invest their time and skills, and the publisher or publishing company invests its capital (money) in the production and distribution of your book with the aim of selling lots of copies and making back their investment.

Book publishing includes: editing, book design and production, but also the relevant expertise in distribution and contact with logistics partners. In return for these services, the publisher receives the majority of your sales, part of the book rights and thus a certain amount of control over your future as an author.

With all the time and effort they commit to making your book a success, the publisher claims an extremely high share of your royalties. In the guidebook sector, for example, a publisher's share can be as much as 90 to 95 per cent. This means that you, as the author, are left with just 5 to 10 percent of the income from book sales. The publisher keeps all the rest and they'll keep taking their percentage for as long as they sell your book.

If your book turns out to be an international bestseller, this is great as there will be plenty of money to go around. However, up to 95 per cent of the total revenue would go into other people's pockets rather than the authors. Given that the publisher has all the upfront costs and have taken a risk this is perhaps understandable, however it can feel like a disadvantage for the author.

Something else to consider if you sign an author's contract, you also hand over a large part of the control to the publisher. You no longer have the sole right to make key decisions about your book, neither about the title design, the overall content, nor how and where your book is marketed. One of

A publisher's share can be as much as 90 to 95 per cent.

our clients, Den, had such a contract and realised part way through writing his manuscript that he wanted to change the original plan and write a different book. Because of the contract he couldn't and had to finish the 'original' book even though he believed there was more value in what he thought it could have evolved into. Obviously, our advice was to keep all of his ideas for a second book; however, it made writing the first one far more challenging without having the freedom to adapt and evolve as he wanted.

This control also extends to distribution. Apart from a few author copies, you won't be able to distribute or sell your book directly. Therefore, you do not know who has bought your book and cannot get in touch with potential customers. Yet it is precisely these distribution opportunities that are an important reason for entrepreneurs, experts and coaches and employees to launch a book in the first place.

Just as knowing what a publisher does is important it is also important to know what they don't do. Many authors argue that the publishing house does the marketing for them and places them in the book trade. Unfortunately, this is not true.

In Germany, Austria and Switzerland, approximately 250,000 books are published each year. Most of them have never been heard of, despite supposedly comprehensive marketing by publishers.

It is true that publishers advertise new titles in their previews, offer review copies to multipliers such as journalists and bloggers and provide bookshops with promotional material. But the bulk of this is for publications by already well-known authors.

The situation is similarly bad when it comes to placing your book in bookshops. The sales space in a shop is very limited. The publisher will primarily display those books from his programme that have the potential to reach the masses, mostly books written by already established authors.

Only when you have invested in your own self-promotion, so you are better known and your book sells better, will you also receive marketing support from your publisher.

Publishers will even urge you to take the initiative in marketing by organising book tours, creating a following and building our audience even before you have a book.

Only when you are better known as an author and the sales figures of your book increase, does the publisher earn money from you by being able to increase the total number of copies sold and thus their return on investment.

But that means that as a relatively unknown author, you always have to do the actual marketing work yourself. In this respect, the belief we mentioned earlier in this section that the publisher does the book marketing for you is invalid.

If you are already well known, you may receive an advance for writing and publishing a book, usually between £1,500 and £4,500. For internationally renowned authors with large print runs or well-established and highly credible experts in a field where a publisher is confident on generating book sales, 6- or 7-figure sums are of course possible. But even best-selling authors are increasingly self-publishing.

In self-publishing, you might not get a book advance but you can actually earn far more whilst still retaining the complete rights and control over your book. As an unknown author, you hardly get any support from publishers. As a well-known author, you don't need them anymore. Like it or not, the publishing companies are going to increasingly struggle over time as more authors realise the benefit of taking control of their own creation and financial future.

> **You can actually earn far more whilst still retaining the complete rights and control over your book.**

SELF-PUBLISHING

The idea that you need a traditional publisher to publish your book and be successful as an author is a myth. A publisher is merely a kind of jury that either accepts or rejects your book.

And this jury does not always judge correctly. Many authors who went on to become best-sellers were first rejected by several publishers. For example, J.K.Rowling was rejected by 12 publishing houses before she finally found a publisher. She has gone on to sell more than 500 million copies of her Harry Potter series and become one of the top 10 bestselling authors of all time. The truth is: the majority of authors with good ideas and good books hope in vain for years to be accepted by a publisher. Yet, most manuscripts are often rejected unread by publishers.

Why is that? It is because publishers work economically and therefore have to forecast the prospect of profits for themselves in each individual case on the basis of various factors. With certain topics and unknown authors, it is clear from the start. The editor doesn't even need to read the manuscript. However, this can lead to some very bad decisions such as the 12 publishers who missed out on producing the Harry Potter phenomenon.

For you as an entrepreneur, a book that would be summarily dismissed by a publisher can still be very lucrative if they use it effectively. As we keep on saying, it is not about the book! We have already shared how we have personally only sold a few thousand copies of all our different books combined and yet made more than half a million pounds to date from using our books as tools to boost our businesses. If we were trying to get published the traditional way, we might still be waiting.

As we keep on saying, it is not about the book!

Therefore, don't be put off and stick to your book idea. If you believe your customers will benefit from your book, you have the opportunity to publish it as an entrepreneur, expert and author. And if you want, with our help.

We created HCB Publishing to help people succeed by helping them use books as the number one tool in their business. Our clients have exciting and instructive stories in their heads, they've gained valuable experience, have enormous knowledge and exciting new ideas and solutions from which their readers can benefit.

Our system, *Your book as a Business Booster* is the modern way to share your message with the world and make the biggest possible impact. To be clear, if you decide it's best to work with us now, or in the future, you'll keep full control, as well as all rights and all income from your book.

Control over your book is also very important from another aspect - the sales process.

You can either market your book through your own website or through a particular landing page. A landing page is simply a one page website that focuses on doign just one thing - in this case, selling your book. The actual sales process could even be linked to your book posting on Amazon, Thalia or another provider. So they handle the printing and shipping etc The special thing about having your own site though is that you will receive your customers' contact details and - provided they agree - you can offer them all manner of extra support and services such as, new publications, newsletters, workshops, seminars, etc now and in the future.

Yes, in the sales process of your book you can even promote further products such as an audio book version shortly before the customer's immediate decision to buy. Extra product offerings like this will increase the size of your sales and therefore increase your profit margins.

In the next chapter we're going to dive more into this component and help you to actually make money from being an author.

CHAPTER 7

These strategies will help you establish yourself as an author

The road to hell is paved with works in progress
- Philip Roth

Unfortunately, most books remain a work in progress. A project people wish they'd finished. For those that do finish, they mistakenly think they are done and remain a work in progress because as we've said once or twice, just having a book isn't enough. This is a common mistake we'd rather you avoid. As we said back at the beginning it is about what you do with your book that is important. The third step of our 3-Step System is 'Profit'. This step is the focus of this chapter so that you can implement the various strategies available and 'Profit' from your book.

When we talk about 'Profit' here we are looking at its broadest definition. The benefit derived from having and using a book effectively for your success. There are a number of different ways to 'use' your book to best effect and you may choose one, some, or all of these to fulfil your vision.

Books convey directly or indirectly your experiences, your personality and your service mentality, perhaps even what it might be like to work with you. People can't help but get to know you as they read what you have written. This is helpful because potential customers learn to trust you as readers and get to know, understand and appreciate your way of thinking. They will either know, like and trust you or they won't. And based on this they will be more or less likely to become customers. Remember when we talked about Marketing as a filter? Well, your book is contributing to this filtering process ensuring you attract more of your ideal customers who are interested in your content and more likely to be open to a next step with you, whatever that might look like.

Unfortunately most people believe that a book will sell itself. They fall into the trap of thinking if it is good enough then people will buy it. Not only is this not true, it is an unhelpful belief pattern that will send you into a spiral of not feeling good enough.

On average, less than 250 copies of each business or non-fiction book are sold each year.

The harsh reality is that very few people make money from book sales. On average, less than 250 copies of each business or non-fiction book are sold each year. And yet, we talked earlier about making hundreds of thousands of pounds from our books. That is because the money is not in the book itself, but rather what people will buy from you as a result of the book; or the promotion or position you can achieve in your career as a result of your book; or perhaps even the staff or funding you can attract because of the way your book is positioning you and your business/expertise. Fundamentally, it isn't about the book but what you sell next.

So, what are you selling next?

Remember we talked about the fact that not everyone will take action from your book, just as we know that not all of you will take action from this book. Rather, you provide an upsell, onsell, order bump, anything that continues to move people forward. Whilst many people are resistant to the concept of sales, all you are actually doing is giving people further opportunities to apply the principles and lessons from your book to their situation. You support people with the next steps or shortcuts and support implementation of whatever it is you do. Effectively, you are giving people the opportunity to skip to the last page or tailor whatever is in the book to them whilst charging a premium for this service. You have already built up trust with them and they know how you work because they have read about the results in your book.So, the key thing you need to do is to get your book into as many hands as possible and then work out what comes next. And before you panic about what comes next, it can be very simple.

In digital or online marketing speak, this strategy is called a 'book funnel', 'tripwire' or 'free + shipping offer'. After you have delivered a valuable and interesting first product (your book), the foundation for a solid business relationship is laid and you can make further offers to your customers.

You can also do this offline by gifting copies of your book to people whom you would like to build a relationship with and then following up. Let's think back to the busy manager as an example of your ideal customer. Of course, you could try to 'cold-call' them and convince them of your business. But how about sending your own book with a personal letter instead? Isn't that far more impressive and more likely to stand out from anyone else in your area?

Whoever you send your book to, recognise that they probably won't read your book in its entirety right away. But they will certainly take a look at the title, the front and back cover, the table of contents, maybe even flip through some chapters and read individual sentences or paragraphs. They will notice and be flattered by the fact that the author of this book is writing to them. How is this going to make them feel about you or the letter you have written?

Understandably, they're going to take you and your correspondence much more seriously because you are writing as an author and proven expert and not as a typical salesman. In contrast to typical give-aways in a classic direct-mailing campaign, your book is a very personal, extremely valuable gift and, what's more, precisely tailored to the recipients' situation.

Perhaps you have also enhanced the book with your personal autograph or a handwritten dedication to the recipient? You'd be amazed at how pleased people are to find a hand-written personal dedication written to them on the inside cover of your book.

In any case, whoever you send your book to, they will keep it or perhaps if it isn't for them, they'll pass it on. In our culture, we simply don't throw books away. Think about it...have you ever thrown a book into the garbage? Charity shop donation, given to a library or homeless shelter, yes. But never straight in the bin! Knowing this, you can be confident your book will stay on someone's desk, even if they never even flip through the pages. Which means when you phone them a few weeks after you've sent them your book, chances are they'll take the time to talk to you.

In our culture, we simply don't throw books away.

So send your book in the post to as many people as possible with a brief letter explaining what you think they'll get out of your book and then call them to check they got your gift and go from there. Remember, this is about Attraction

Marketing (Attention and Curiosity) and who doesn't like free gifts?

There are many variations as to how you can effectively onsell or upsell using your book and here are some examples:

COACHING OR CONSULTING

Marie Kondo, Japanese entrepreneur and author, for example, developed the "KonMari Method" and wrote the book *Magic Cleaning: How Tidying Up the Right Way Changes Your Life.*

In the book she shows readers how to clean up their living environment in a special way and thus lead a happier and more relaxed life. The book has sold millions of copies worldwide. Today, she also advises people in her KonMari method and even offers certifications so that others can learn her method and become independent advisors. So with just one book, she has created wealth for herself and others who have learnt her methods and get paid to implement them and also improved the life experience of all of those who have implemented her changes. Yes, this particular book would have made money through sales royalties, however, the much more significant wealth was in the upsell and onsell opportunity.

We talked initially about how visible 'experts' are now and potentially how commonplace. However, with a book that outlines your system and way of working, supported by the experiences of your clients, you will be able to stand out from your competitors when selling your advice, guidance, coaching or the like. People will want to work with you and most importantly they will pay to do that.It works similarly if you work in groups. Entrepreneur Joe Polish is the founder of one of the most exclusive 'masterminds' in the world, the so-called '25K Group'. Annual membership costs 25,000 euros. In this mastermind, millionaires and billionaires meet to exchange new business strategies. With the aim of acquiring new clients for his '25K Group', he has published *The Little Book of Asskickers*. In this book, Polish gives his readers various tips and insights from his years as an entrepreneur whilst promoting his group, which has raised his profile and attracted many new prospects.

Tony Robbins, one of the best known speakers in the personal development world has written numerous books to promote his content and provide another option for people who can't work with him 1:1, whilst generally supporting and building his credibility.

SELLING INFORMATION PRODUCTS

One of our clients, Richard from Bristol, has implemented the book *The Ultimate Funnel Business* and has already sold over 55,000 copies. He offers his bound book to customers for about £5 and in return they get over 160 pages of concentrated funnel knowledge. After buying his book, the reader receives further offers, including offers for courses from Richard that are all delivered online through his own funnel.If you offer courses or other information products, this strategy is quite effective. This is because the first barrier to doing business with you is extremely low, as you are offering a low-cost starter product.

SELLING PHYSICAL, TANGIBLE PRODUCTS

US entrepreneur Dave Asprey is the founder of the Bulletproof Diet and has built up a multi-million dollar empire with the help of his book *The Bulletproof Diet*.

In his guidebook, he describes how to burn fat by taking a special coffee mix in the morning. Of course, in his online shop he sells exactly the ingredients that are necessary for this high-quality coffee mix: 'Bulletproof Coffee' and 'Brain Octane Oil'.

First, Asprey explains in his book how his diet principle works and what needs to be considered. In this way, he motivates his readers to buy the products from his online shop. In this way, Asprey turns a book buyer who only spent a minimal amount on his book into a loyal customer who buys his products for years and earns him many times the book margin in sales. The beauty of this is that the coffee mix purchase is recurring. This would also apply to supplements or other foodstuffs.

Similarly, there are many exercise professionals who have produced a book to sell their equipment. Whilst there isn't the same recurring revenue opportunity here, the next 'product' will always be a larger investment increasing the amount you earn per client and strengthening your relationship with them so that whatever you next sell is more likely to be something they will be buying.

SELLING SOFTWARE

Russel Brunson is an online marketer from the USA and the inventor of the 'ClickFunnels' software. In his book *Dotcom Secrets*, he shows his readers various ways of selling their products using online marketing.

In doing so, Brunson refers to concrete sales funnels and what one should consider when designing, creating and using them. In his explanations, he also repeatedly points out that the funnels described can easily be implemented with the help of his software.His book was a great success. As a result, Brunson was able to win thousands of new customers for his software and his popularity amnd income increased immensely.

BECOME A SPEAKER

Entrepreneur Eric Ries is a software developer and founder of the start-up IMVU, a 3D chat community. While building this start-up, he and his team accidentally found a programming method that allowed them to save a lot of time and money in product development: Lean Development/Customer Development.

Based on this method, Ries wrote the book *The Lean Start-up* and thus launched a gigantic movement.

Today, almost every founder knows the terms MVP (Minimum Viable Product) and 'Lean development'. Eric Ries' book has contributed significantly to this awareness. In his lectures and training sessions, he explains to his audience how to run a lean company. Interestingly, Ries' method was not new at all; it actually came from Toyota. But Ries introduced it to a new target group and, as a result, became successful.

There are many other examples of authors who have created a 'book tour' from their books to get in front of more people. The speaking itself could be the end game, or yet another opportunity to sell 1:1 services or other products. Similarly, your book could be a free giveaway for anyone who attends your talk or workshop so they have immediate super high-value content to take with them. This gives you a reason for you to follow up with them and perhaps see if they might become your next private client.

Who knows, you may even launch your presidential campaign with a book? Barack Obama, the first black US President, certainly did. No one knew who he was until he published his first book, *Dreams from My Father*, and there is/was a lot of speculation about whether Michelle Obama was following a similar path with her book *Becoming*. We'll wait and see...

You may even launch your presidential campaign with a book?

ATTRACTING NEW EMPLOYEES

Tony Hsieh is the founder of the online shop Zappos. In his book *Delivering Happiness: The Path to Profit, Passion and Purpose* he described his path to becoming a successful entrepreneur. Furthermore, in his book Hsieh also presents his unique company culture: the company does not offer its employees a conventional workplace, but a home.

The various extraordinary facets of the company and its culture are described in detail. With his book, Hsieh has achieved several goals simultaneously: he positions himself as a successful entrepreneur with a unique company culture. He demonstrates to his customers how much they, too, are valued thanks to this special spirit. And of course, readers learn how fantastic it is to work at Zappos. In this way, Zappos has created its very own recruiting channel. Only very few companies use this. A book could also be a brilliant way for recruiters to get in touch with top candidates.

START A MOVEMENT

With over 5 billion copies sold, the Bible is the best-selling book of all time - by a gigantic margin over all other books. And, do you know what all the religions of the world have in common? They all started with a holy scripture or codex - in other words, a book. Every great movement and every great thought needed a solid foundation to spread.

Maybe your book could also change the world...

You need to dig deeper and deeper into the various facets you stand for and the content you believe in. There is no better medium for this task than a book. Maybe your book could also change the world...

GET EXCLUSIVE INVESTMENT OPPORTUNITIES

Gerald Hörhan is an entrepreneur, investor and moreover known as the 'Investment Punk'. With his identically named book, *Investment Punk: Why You Work and We Get Rich*, he has secured a first-class position as a provocative financial expert.

In his book, he describes frequent mistakes people make when it comes to finances and shows how one should think and act instead. As a result, he is not only perceived as a financial genius, but also receives a lot of approval from wealthy people who share his views. Thanks to his fame, he not only gains readers and fans, but also gets new clients plus exclusive investment deals.

With all of these amazing options to use your book as a platform for better, bigger or different relationships, a job, promotion, clients and sales, it is very apparent that it isn't about the book but what you do with it. That said, you still need a book to be able to do all of this, so if any or all of these possibilities excite you, fantastic. Hopefully, this will provide you with some impetus to get started. If you haven't yet sorted out your idea and structure, go back to Chapter 4 and start with the end in mind, follow the system and start creating some of these amazing possibilities for yourself and for your business.

CHAPTER 8

Next Steps

A book is a dream you hold in your hand
- Neil Gailman

Congratulations! You have made it. You now know the advantages of becoming an author and most importantly what you need to do to create your book and how to use it for success! We want your dream to become a reality, something that you can hold in your hand. That is one of the many reasons we wrote this book. Yes, we enjoy writing books and, yes, we know the impact they have for us, AND more importantly, we know the impact they will have for you when you take action and create your book.

We have set out many examples of how you could grow your business or career through your book and given you a clear order to do things in. However, in many ways we've only just scratched the surface. Once you start taking action, things will change and you'll need to re-read and re-apply different components. Learning and growing is a never-ending process, so keep reflecting on what you need to move you forward to the next phase and perhaps this book can be a portable cheerleader and coach to keep you going.

> **Your ideas, your thoughts and your words have the chance to outlive you and change lives.**

Whether it's a new job, promotion, marketing, recruitment or starting a movement, having your own book will exponentially increase your results in all areas. It amplifies all your activities and efforts through an increase in authority and credibility.

Your ideas, your thoughts and your words have the chance to outlive you and change lives. Even after your death, your book can still reach people, touch them and change them. You don't have to be an academic, a gifted scientist or an experienced copywriter to publish your own book. You don't even have to make it to the Top Whatever Best-Selling list. You just have to reach your target audience.

> **Simply choose whether you want to benefit from being an author or not.**

Simply choose whether you want to benefit from being an author or not. Status, more authority, dream clients and more sales - all this and more is in your hands alone and you have to choose whether to put in the work to make it happen or not.

The difference between successful people and those who spend their lives dreaming of success lies in the choices they make. So, as we said at the beginning of the book, you have 3 choices...

Remember to persist long enough to get to the end so you can move to the final stage of our system: Profit!

The first is to choose not to be an author and if this is you that's ok. However, we are sure that someone else in your life might want what's possible from being an author, so please pass this book on to them.

The second choice is that you will have already started on your book, you will have answered questions, maybe even sorted out your book architecture and you're off and racing. Just keep going! If you find yourself struggling going it alone for whatever reason, perhaps you need to swap to option 3 where we can help you shortcut your journey or at least ensure your success. Whether you are just starting out or you are part way through your project or you have even finished your book, we are able to support you. Either way, remember to persist long enough to get to the end so you can move to the final stage of our system: Profit!

Option 3 is where we work together to help you become a high earning and highly successful author. Simply give us a call or email and we can explore how best we may work together and move your project forward. We admit that we used to think getting support was a sign of weakness. Now, however, we realise how short life is and how many successful people take the 'smart' route of enlisting support. There are very few 'self-made' anythings in this world, as when you scratch beneath the surface you realise how many people have enlisted support to ensure their success.

When our clients work with us, they invest only about 90 days of their time and only about 90 working hours in their entire book project. Our team will take care of all the exhausting details, which normally last about 4 to 5 months. When you think about what getting your book 'out' will achieve and all of the other things that you can be doing whilst others get on with it, it tends to be a bit of a 'no brainer'.

Regardless of which option represents where you are now or where you may end up, you now have 3 steps to get you to your success: Prepare, Persist and Profit. And more than that, you have started a journey using our overall success system of business: Knowledge, Mindset and Community.

Step 1: Knowledge.

This book is packed with as much great information as possible, so you have the tools to write a book and use it for your success whatever stage it and you are at. We have focused on teaching you the right things in the right order so you know what to do and more importantly how and when to do it. As most experts and practitioners have never been trained how to make money from their expertise, it's unsurprising that so many struggle in business. We start with the right foundations and build up to more advanced strategies once the basics are in place. If you're already further along and have a book, congratulations! However, we find that most authors or would-be authors share the same basic challenges, so you'll enjoy even greater success by focusing first on the fundamentals.

Step 2: Mindset.

The right mindset enables you to take action and use the knowledge you have. We have gone through many of the limiting beliefs you may have around writing a book, let alone doing anything with it. Acknowledging that self-sabotage exists is the first step, followed by working out how you can best upgrade your mindset so it works for you rather than against you. This is why we have shared lots of stories from our clients to help you realise that if they can do it, so can you. We have also shared our own challenges and failures so you can see how we overcame them and how you could do this in your own life.

Step 3: Community.

When it comes to a supportive community, most of us don't necessarily have people who talk us up. Instead, most people are surrounded by people who talk them down, even if only unconsciously. We would, however, suggest that you take a good look at who you have surrounded yourself with as some of our most 'supportive' family and friends are so committed to keeping us safe that they keep us stuck. Having a peer group who share your values and are similarly driven to succeed, is one of the key reasons our clients grow and succeed so quickly.

If you don't have a supportive community or you perhaps need to augment the one you have, we would encourage you to join ours. Sharing challenges and successes with other growth-orientated heart centred people will accelerate your journey even faster.

https://www.facebook.com/groups/
HeartCentredBusiness/

Now, as proud as we are of this book, we have to reluctantly admit, there's no way it can contain all the answers to every situation you're going to encounter as you Prepare, Persist and Profit from your book. If you want to further accelerate your journey, take advantage now of a FREE Coaching Call with one of our Book Coaching Team (valued at £1000).

By now, you're aware of the difference the right support can make and we'd love to fast-track your journey to success. We promise this free Book Coaching Call will give you 3 things:

1. You'll get energised, motivated and have a clear plan of action.
2. You'll have clarity on whether a book could help your career or business and what type of book might suit you best.
3. We'll explore if we're a match to work together to make your book, career or business goals a reality.

If we're a match to work together, we'll get started right away. If we're not a match, we'll advise what other types of support might be a better fit for you.

Visit www. hcbpublishing.com/ book/offers to book your free call.

Whether it's best we work together now, or not, the call is FREE and you'll find it massively powerful! However, our Coaching Team has limited time, so this call is only for you if you are serious about growing your career or business and want our support in making that happen.

Please now visit www.hcbpublishing.com/book/offers to book your free call.

We would of course love to hear what difference this book has made for you so please share your success stories with us so we can celebrate with you.

Connect with us via our public Facebook Group https://www.facebook.com/groups/HeartCentredBusiness

Via email hello@hcbpublising.com

Or via phone +44 (0)333 987 4245

The world needs your expertise and is waiting for you to write, publish and market your book. We're excited to be on this journey with you and thank you for making a bigger difference in the world!

David, Chris, Karene and the HCB Publishing Team.

About the
Authors

DAVID GIL CRISTÓBAL

Serial Entrepreneur and co-founder of The Collection by HCB, David Gil Cristóbal turns people into brands. By putting the correct business systems and structures in place for scalable success, David's clients become the go-to experts in their industry. He has spent more than 3 decades in the sports and business arena, which includes a career as a professional footballer, creating and selling one of Switzerland's top health & fitness organisations, and launching Fitness Fortune University, which builds elite fitness businesses in as little as 90 days.

David's transformative journey started with a simple question after being 'retired' age 33 from the football community, "What now for the next 60 years?". He shares with passion and honesty the highs and lows that pro sports & business has in common, his experiences as a high-performing athlete and how – and why – he had no choice other than to radically change his path and find a new mission once his football career came to a close. David is an outstanding example of what life can look like as a committed, disciplined and purposefully business owner after you find your inner self and clear mission.

He has personally trained more than 1,000 companies to scale their businesses. The events surrounding the pandemic found him busier than ever, as he put his heart and soul into keeping his fitness industry colleagues and clients afloat.

David, Chris and Karene co-founded The Collection by HCB where their multiple companies are on a mission to create 1,000 heart centred millionaires. David holds a Master's degree in Business Management and Leadership, has built multiple 6 and 7-figure businesses, spoken to more than 100,000 people at business and financial conferences in 13 different countries and on 3 different continents. Spending time with business titans including Sir Richard Branson, Kevin Harrington, Robert Kiyosaki, Tony Robbins. He is the best-selling author of 7 books in 2 different languages – he himself speaks 6 languages, and has even starred in a film.

CHRIS LAMBERT-GORWYN

Chris has been at rock bottom. With more than £100,000 of debt and his first child on the way, he knew something had to change – and fast. He was working every waking hour to provide for his family but it wasn't working. His transformative journey started with attending a single sales seminar (which he won't mind telling you, he was very reluctant to attend) and having his eyes opened to what was possible in a heart centred business. He went from a dark financial hole to never having to work another day for money in his life.

Chris and his wife Karene have built multiple 6 and 7-figure companies, written numerous #1 best-selling business and personal development books and founded the UK's leading business training company, Heart Centred Business. This flagship company forms the heart of The Collection by HCB and is where the collective mission of creating 1,000 heart centred millionaires was born and started gathering momentum.

Humbled by numerous awards, Chris has spoken at business conferences in 14 different countries, spending time with business titans including Sir Richard Branson, Les Brown, Baroness Michelle Mone, Kevin Harrington, Robert Kiyosaki, Tony Robbins and Randi Zuckerberg.

Accolades aside, Chris speaks with passion and candid honesty about both his successes and his failures. Open about his challenges in life and business, he credits a lot of his success to the battle he fought with cancer as a teenager and even goes so far as to say it was one of the best things that ever happened to him.

Chris is the proud husband of Karene and together with their daughter Mya and maltipoo puppy Goldie, they recently achieved his dream of moving his family from central London to live by the beach on the south coast of England.

KARENE LAMBERT-GORWYN

Karene had it all – the money, the title and the status. An incredibly successful corporate career saw her working with numerous multi-national organisations including BMW, BP, ITV as well as the Singapore and UK government, all before she'd even blown out the candles on her 30th birthday cake.

But following a severe accident that left her unable to work for some time, she started to question whether she was on the right path. So, she left it all behind and forged an entirely new way forward, from scratch.

Karene now once again has it all – but better. Because now she not only has a multi-million-dollar property portfolio that pays her income each month whether she works or not; she also has balance, health, freedom and meaningful relationships.

Alongside husband Chris, she's built multiple 6 and 7-figure companies, co-founded The Collection by HCB and Heart Centred Business, the UK's leading business training company. Through this, they share the systems they used to get themselves where they are today, without sacrificing the things that really matter. And it works. Just ask the 3,000+ business owners who have gone on to thrive after implementing their systems.

These systems have taken Karene from tea at 10 Downing Street to dinner at the House of Lords. She has presented at conferences around the world, rubbing shoulders with Robert and Kim Kiyosaki, Randy Zuckerberg, Baroness Michelle Mone and Baroness Karen Brady – to name but a few – and has written numerous business and personal development #1 best-selling books.

Karene shares with passion and honesty the highs – and lows – of business, her experiences as a high-flying woman and how – and why – she chose to change her path. And what life can look like as a business owner, mummy and all those other roles that we pick up along the way.

Focused on what works rather than what's popular, The Collection by HCB is a growing group of companies with the shared mission of creating 1,000 heart centred millionaires.

Sharing resources, expertise and a passion for improving people and businesses, Chris, Karene and David are actively looking for business partners to add to the heart centred collection.

Do you have the skills, the passion, or a business that could impact the world?

For an interview to partner with Chris, Karene and David and join the Collection by HCB, email hello@hcb-collection.com

Website: www.hcb-collection.com
Email: hello@hcb-collection.com
Phone: +44 (0)333 987 4245

We're on a mission to create 1,000 heart centred millionaires

Would you like to be one of them?

At Heart Centred Business we typically work with women in their 40's who are running their own 6-figure business, working all hours and doing everything for not enough profit.

We help them grow their business to 7 figures so it can run with or without them and they can reclaim their life outside of work.

For a free Business Growth Session to explore how best to move your business forward, visit:

Website: www.heartcentredbusiness.com/free-strat-call
Email: hello@heartcentredbusiness.com
Phone: +44 (0)333 987 4245

Fewer than 1% of the population will ever write a book.

And most authors rarely make any money from their books.

So why do it?!

Your book is the most effective marketing tool for your business or career if used effectively.

But, it's not about the book!

At HCB Publishing we'll help you write a best-selling book, and more importantly, we'll help you use your book to make money.

Most of our authors start making money before they've finished writing their book. We focus on what works, rather than what's popular.

Want to know more, email us at hello@hcbpublishing.com and have a free Book Strategy Session to explore how a book could help your business or career.

Website: www.hcbpublishing.com
Email: hello@hcbpublishing.com
Phone: +44 (0) 333 987 4245

Words THAT Work

Business success powered by great content

We create content that tells your clients exactly what they need to know, in exactly the way you want it to be said.

This is content that gets tangible results, fast.

Be seen by the right people

Connect with your ideal target audience

Dramatically increase your sales

To explore how better words could transform your business, email the Words That Work Team now on hello@wordsthatwork.uk for a free Strategy Consultation on your content.

Website: www.wordsthatwork.uk
Email: hello@wordsthatwork.uk
Phone: +44 (0) 203 432 7050

Be seen, be heard
Get paid what you're worth

What if, whenever you talked, people sat up and listened?

What if you were connected to your presence and power so you could make significantly more money?

From 30+ years of experience, we've found there are 3 key steps to making this happen...

Step 1 is creating presence and confidence in your own body and your own voice

Step 2 is to become a good public speaker

Step 3 is the essential step most people never take...learn how to profit speak. The art of making money and getting paid whenever you present.

If you want to be seen, be heard and get paid what you're worth, email hello@speaktoshine.uk now and we'll explore how these 3 steps could work for you.

Website: www.speaktoshine.co.uk
Email: hello@speaktoshine.co.uk
Phone: +44 (0) 203 740 5939

Here's to good health!

The best investment you'll ever make

The key to good health is recovery. Yet we neglect this essential component because we're all too busy pushing through in order to create better results.

> "Don't tell me to do less.
> Help me recover quicker and
> perform better so I can do more!"

Be Fueled with the right nutrition and effortlessly build recovery and better performance into every day.

To experience this yourself and enjoy an exclusive discount, visit...website.....

Website: www.befueld.co.uk
Email: support@befueld.co.uk
Phone: +44 (0)333 987 4245

Bored of doing the same old job and want to do something more interesting?

Would you like to be paid a 6-figure income for changing people's lives?

We've trained thousands of people to succeed with clients from more than 100 different professions. Whatever your life skills or professional background, we can help you develop world-class coaching skills AND teach you how to build a successful and highly lucrative coaching career.

To register your interest in this upcoming training, visit..... website...

Website: www.hcbcoaching.com
Email: hello@hcbcoaching.com
Phone: +44 (0)333 987 4245

A platform for all your marketing needs & business growth

Do you need more clients?

Does your business keep going through feast and famine?

Frustrated with the day-to-day hassle of running your own business?

Most business owners are experts at what they do with their clients, not at building and running a successful business.

HCB HUB allows you to focus on what matters - connecting with your clients.

From customised lists of potential clients, to step-by-step daily actions ensuring a consistent stream of high paying clients coming into your business.

To systemise your business and open up an unlimited client flow, email hello@hcb-hub.com for exclusive discounts to a system will transform your business and your income forever.

Website: www.hcb-hub.com
Email: hello@hcb-hub.com
Phone: +44 (0)333 987 4245

Additional
Publications

FROM FITNESS TO FORTUNE (2018)

The health and fitness industry has experienced exponential growth over the past decade. With *From Fitness To Fortune*, David Gil Cristóbal offers his readers an in-depth examination of the steps necessary to create and expand a top fitness business.

From Fitness To Fortune is the successful fitness entrepreneur David's legacy to his industry: 'A book for those who, like me, are willing to go to great lengths to get to the elite level', says David. 'It's really not easy to build a successful business. And it's even harder to keep it alive for the long haul.' In this book, the professional athlete and multiple business owner's experiences blend into a proven, sustainable recipe for fitness entrepreneurs. Get your business fit! What could be more inspiring than advancing the healthy lives of thousands of people?

Available on Amazon or to get a free copy visit: www.hcbpublishing.com/published-books

REAL ESTATE CROWDFUNDING BOOK: THE NEW FORM OF REAL ESTATE INVESTMENT (2019)

Few investment areas are as lucrative as real estate. The real estate market is therefore booming even in times of crisis. Interest rates are unbelievably low. The best time to invest.

Crowdfunding offers completely new possibilities for financing. The international businessman David Gil Cristóbal has recognised this and used it for himself. In his book *Real Estate Crowdfunding - The New Form of Real Estate Investment*, he offers his readers detailed help in deciding whether and for whom this new form of financing is suitable. He explains the basic concept, warns against the common scams of the fraudsters and shows how surplus funds can be specifically turned into a profitable investment. A book for all those who are looking for new low-risk investment opportunities far away from the stock market.

Available on Amazon or to get a free copy visit: www.hcbpublishing.com/published-books

NEW MINDSET - NEW YOU
(2019)

Nothing is more inspiring than trust, both for us and for the people around us. The power of believing in ourselves opens doors to new plans, enriches and overcomes deep fears. In his book *New Mindset - New You*, the award-winning author David Gil Cristóbal explores how powerful and life-changing the feeling of confidence can be.

Each chapter is a journey to the inner self for his readers with the goal of improving their self-image and finally living the life they dream of. David's guide uses a 7-day mindset series to develop an actionable and replicable approach to actively working on one's life through one's state of consciousness, to become happier and more inspiring to others. Do you also want to fundamentally change your way of thinking? Then perhaps David Gil Cristóbal's new mindset and his 7-day course will be the start of quite a new life.

Available on Amazon or to get a free copy visit: www.hcbpublishing.com/published-books

LOSE WEIGHT – BUT WITHOUT A DIET (2020)

Haven't you always wanted to know the 'basic laws' of losing weight? Apart from all the fashionable diets, David Gil Cristóbal creates a very essential foundation in this book, which, beyond all the approaches and theories that are constantly springing up, starts with our consciousness, our heart and our head.

'I wanted to contribute something to the topic of losing weight without promoting any supposed miracle cures like many others and without the very ephemeral fashionable touch of most diets', the former professional athlete and successful fitness entrepreneur explains his intention. 'After all, I don't want to go down in history as just another diet charlatan, I really want to help', says David. His way offers people lasting, practicable and everyday help for self-help. The English word 'diet' already contains one of David's central pillars for weight reduction - a healthier dietary principle as the basis and goal of any weight loss. With this book you will become much lighter!

Available on Amazon or to get a free copy visit: www.hcbpublishing.com/published-books

Grow Your Heart Centred Business
From Passion to Profit (2020)
Chris & Karene Lambert-Gorwyn

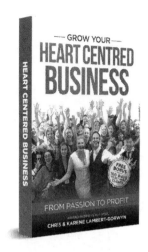

Would you like to grow your business?

What if you could get paid more for doing the work you love?

This book will show you how.

Step-by-step actionable advice for going from startup to £250,000, Chris and Karene share their experience, strategies and wisdom in one-of-a-kind business bible.

Sharing candidly about their successes and failures, Chris and Karene are on a mission to create 1,000 heart centred millionaires. This book is your first step to making that happen.

Available on Amazon or to get a free copy visit: www. heartcentredbusiness.com/book

Back Pain
21 Secrets to Resolving Back
Pain (2020)
Chris & Karene Lambert-Gorwyn and David Gil Cristobal

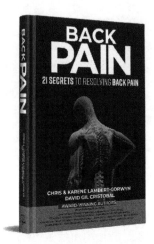

In collaboration with:

Yves De Vos, Emma Grace, Dr Andrea Haas, Gary Jones, Claudia R. Knights, Christine Laidlaw, Jane McDowell, Miriam Moffat, Lisa Moore, Sean Moseley, Stephen Parkus, Irma Prins, Beth Redfern, Karen Revivo, Simon Rogers, Mark Roughley, Adam Sealey, Gordon Sharp, Graham Stones

Imagine what it would be like to not wake up with back pain?

This book brings together some of the foremost experts in the UK, and by following the advice they provide in this book, it is not only possible to reduce your back pain, it's actually very likely.

Available on Amazon or to get a free copy visit: www.hcbpublishing.com/published-books

Confidence
How to have it and how to
keep it (2020)
Chris & Karene Lambert-Gorwyn and David Gil Cristóbal

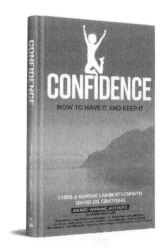

In collaboration with:

Jules Francis, Anna Goodwin, Emma Grace, Dr Andrea Haas, Anni Jakenfelds, Lisa Moore, Molly Jones, Mats Kolbjornsen, Christine Laidlaw, Mike Lawrence, Jane McDowell, Irma Prins, Simon Rogers, David Roylance, Sophie Thwaites.

Confidence is that special ingredient that makes everything work better. Bringing together advice usually reserved for high-paying clients, this book will give you insights, inspiration and, most importantly, action steps you can take right now so you can make a difference in your life today.

Available on Amazon or to get a free copy visit: www.hcbpublishing.com/published-books

Energy
How to unleash your inner fire (2020)
Chris & Karene Lambert-Gorwyn and David Gil Cristóbal

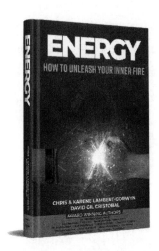

In collaboration with:

Lucy Ascham, Kate Gare, Anna Goodwin, Emma Grace, Dr Andrea Haas, Karl Hutchinson, Pauline Kirtley, Claudia R. Knights, Christine Laidlaw, Jane McDowell, Hazel Macfarlane, Lisa Moore, Irma Prins, Simon Rogers, Tara Sutton, Sarah Hamon-Watt

If you had more energy, you'd be able to do more, concentrate more, work more and live more. Very simply, more energy means more chance of success in every area of life.

This book brings together some of the best experts in the UK at creating energy so you can start changing your life today.

Available on Amazon or to get a free copy visit: www.hcbpublishing.com/published-books

*The year the world changed
How to survive and thrive in
uncertain times* (2021)
**Chris and Karene Lambert-
Gorwyn and David Gil
Cristóbal**

In collaboration with:

Alice Cooke, Anna Goodwin,
Amy Rogers, David Roylance,
Jane McDowell, Sarah Hamon-
Watt, Sharon Betterton

Let's face it, the Covid pandemic sucked!

But like everything in life, there are always things to learn
no matter how hard the circumstances.

This book is a collection of what the Heart Centred Business
team learned during the pandemic and how they manage to
set themselves up personally and professionally for success
so you can do the same.

Available on Amazon or to get a free copy visit:
www.hcbpublishing.com/published-books

Printed in Great Britain
by Amazon